SHAKESPEARE IN MONTANA

Shakespeare
IN **MONTANA**

BIG SKY COUNTRY'S LOVE AFFAIR WITH
THE WORLD'S MOST FAMOUS WRITER

GRETCHEN E. MINTON

UNIVERSITY OF NEW MEXICO PRESS | ALBUQUERQUE

Library of Congress Cataloging-in-Publication Data
Names: Minton, Gretchen E., 1970– author.
Title: Shakespeare in Montana: Big Sky Country's love affair with the world's most
famous writer / Gretchen E. Minton.
Description: Albuquerque: University of New Mexico Press, 2020. |
Includes bibliographical references and index.
Identifiers: LCCN 2019053551 (print) | LCCN 2019053552 (e-book) |
ISBN 9780826361561 (paperback) | ISBN 9780826361578 (e-book)
Subjects: LCSH: Shakespeare, William, 1564–1616—Appreciation—Montana. |
Shakespeare, William, 1564–1616—Stage history—Montana. |
Theater—Montana—History.
Classification: LCC PR3105.M56 2020 (print) | LCC PR3105 (e-book) |
DDC 792.09786—dc23
LC record available at https://lccn.loc.gov/2019053551
LC e-book record available at https://lccn.loc.gov/2019053552

Cover illustrations courtesy of Vecteezy.com
Designed by Felicia Cedillos
Composed in Bembo Std 10/35/14.25

For Kevin,
who taught me about the American West,
who told me about the mountain men,
who researched in advance of me as well as by my side,
who drove me across our vast state time and again,
who pictured this project both metaphorically and literally,
who made it possible, in every way, for me to write these words.

CONTENTS

ILLUSTRATIONS

ACKNOWLEDGMENTS

When I was offered a tenure-track position in the English Department at Montana State University in 2006, I felt like I had won the lottery: I would be pursuing the only career I had ever wanted in a state I had always appreciated for its natural beauty. At that time, however, I never imagined that my research on Shakespeare would have any special relationship to the state that would be my new home. It was my husband, Kevin Brustuen, who first told me that the mountain men of the nineteenth century were avid readers of Shakespeare, which prompted me to wonder how and why Shakespeare has a rich history in this state, beginning with the first white explorers of this region and continuing to the present with Montana Shakespeare in the Parks.

This book reflects over a decade of exploration as Kevin and I ranged over Montana's archives, newspapers, libraries, towns, landscapes, and communities in order to understand the story of Shakespeare in Montana. Over the course of these years many people and institutions have assisted in bringing this book to its completion, and although I do not have sufficient space to name each individual, I would like to acknowledge the most significant of these contributions.

Grant funding from Humanities Montana, MSU, and the Ivan Doig Center for the Study of the Lands and Peoples of the North American West was crucial for travel, archive visits, and research support. This funding also allowed me to hire two exceptional research assistants: Chase Templet uncovered valuable resources and completed the Index, and Abby Lake also dedicated herself to this project in ways that proved invaluable. I also owe a debt of gratitude to all of the archivists and librarians who have provided assistance along the way, especially those at the Montana Historical Society, Butte-Silver Bow archives, the Dillon Public Library, Fort Benton's historical research center, the Ursuline Academy, and MSU.

MSIP is not only the inspiration for the first and last chapters of this book but an organization full of current and past actors, directors, and staff who have given me a great deal of insight into this remarkable cultural treasure. I wish to thank Kevin Asselin, and especially Susan Miller, for providing access to the MSIP archives, information about the company's history, and help in locating and identifying many photos. MSU photographer Adrian Sanchez Gonzalez also graciously enhanced some old prints that serve as a window into past performances.

Several colleagues at MSU have enhanced my understanding of the American West, including Susan Kollin, Linda Karell, and Jan Zauha. The two external readers of the *Shakespeare in Montana* manuscript were Mary Murphy (a historian from MSU) and Paul Prescott (a Shakespearean from the University of Warwick). Both were generous and thorough with their feedback, which inspired and challenged me to expand and revise the book, and I appreciate that their suggestions have made this a better work than it would have been otherwise. In the final stages of revision, I was lucky enough to have one more thorough reading from Heather Easterling (Gonzaga University).

I have given public lectures on much of this material, and each presentation to an audience has enabled me to rethink and revise in productive ways. For these opportunities, I am grateful to Linda Woodbridge, Bob Mokwa, Nicol Rae, Mark Vessey, and Mike Cok (Mike and Kathy Cok additionally gave me the ideal writer's retreat in Big Sky). An early version of the chapter on women's reading groups appeared in an essay collection entitled *Women Making Shakespeare* (Bloomsbury, 2013). Finally, my gratitude goes to the production staff at the University of New Mexico Press for working with me throughout the publication process, especially the senior acquisitions editor, Elise McHugh.

Shakespeare in Montana is dear to me because it represents the perfect marriage between my favorite author and my favorite state. I've told several people that I would follow up this book with one that tells the story of what it was like to write it—a story of research and road trips that Kevin and I took (usually with our son, Luke, an ever-eager participant in literal and metaphorical journeys) in order to better understand Montana and its multifaceted fascination with Shakespeare. I won't write such a book, of course, but if I did it would be full of anecdotes about the Montana landscapes we traveled through, but even more about the many fascinating Montanans that we have talked to along the way.

The dedication of this book could never have been to anyone but Kevin. There is as much of him in these pages as there is of me. To say that I am grateful for everything he has given to *Shakespeare in Montana*, but especially to Luke and me, would be the most ridiculous of understatements.

PREFACE

There lies your way, due west.

—*Twelfth Night*

I was waiting in line to check in to a resort hotel in Whitefish, Montana, when the friendly and talkative manager welcomed me and asked the purpose of my visit. As we stood in the lobby with the typical Montana decor—rustic wooden furniture, a large fireplace, displays of stuffed and mounted animals—I told him I would be giving a talk about Shakespeare, and he posed a series of questions that made it clear he had very little knowledge about the author to whom I had dedicated my life's work. The question he asked that initially shocked me the most was: "Where was he from? Was he American?" While most people of course would immediately answer in the way I did ("No, he was English . . . "), now that I reflect upon the question, it's more interesting than I at first thought. While William Shakespeare, who was born in 1564 in Stratford-upon-Avon, was most certainly English, "Shakespeare," which is the sum total of his works and cultural influence, has long since come to be recognized as a global phenomenon.

The United States, a country founded upon rejecting most things English, nonetheless adopted Shakespeare as its own. James Fenimore Cooper, one of the earliest voices of a distinctively "American" literature that romanticized life on the frontier, famously asserted that Shakespeare was "the great author of America."[1] As that frontier shifted ever westward, it was in fact Shakespeare that the restless settlers carried with them, both physically and metaphorically. As Virginia Mason Vaughan and Alden Vaughan write in their book

Shakespeare in America, Shakespeare was demonstrably "the favorite playwright at almost every location on the moving frontier."[2]

This phenomenon has been endlessly fascinating to scholars and journalists alike, thus there are several books on Shakespeare in America and several articles and occasional monographs dedicated specifically to the popularity of Shakespeare in the American West.[3] Such works abound with a fascinating array of anecdotes about unlikely encounters between mountain men such as Jim Bridger and the stories of Shakespeare. When I learned of such stories, I was equally fascinated, but I also wanted to understand something more about Shakespeare's place in my own corner of the West. Although others have asserted that "Shakespeare's popularity in the American West dwindled as the West was settled and ceased to be wild,"[4] the history in Montana suggests something different: a prolonged and multifaceted fascination with the words and works of the quintessential English author.

Shakespeare in Montana focuses on the people and lands of this Northern Rockies region, but it does not limit its chronological scope to the nineteenth century. Indeed, much of the vibrant Shakespeare culture in Montana took place at the turn of the twentieth century, and the love affair between residents of this region and Shakespeare's works has not waned even in the twenty-first century. A case in point is a book entitled *State by State: A Panoramic Portrait of America* (2008), which features a map of the country with icons to epitomize what each state is known for. Iowa has an ear of corn, Arizona a cactus, Kentucky a racehorse, and so on. Surprisingly, Montana is emblazoned with Shakespeare's face. Why? "If there is one thing all Montanans have in common, other than a disdain for speed limits and a thing for huckleberries, it is a love of William Shakespeare."[5] This unexpected statement is prompted by the popularity of Montana Shakespeare in the Parks (MSIP), which has had a profound impact upon the state's cultural scene since its inception in 1973. For this reason, *Shakespeare in Montana* begins with a prologue that situates Montana's love of Shakespeare in the present, explaining the five-decade odyssey of MSIP's actors to the most remote area of the state. After this prologue that attests to the continued fascination that Montanans have with Shakespeare, *Shakespeare in Montana* takes up the journey with the earliest mountain men in this region, then proceeds in a rough chronological fashion, but with overlapping and doubling back that allows for connections across decades and regions of the state. Some shorter pieces of the story that do not fit naturally into the larger narratives are told separately, as interludes between the chapters.

Shakespeare in Montana is necessarily full of anecdotes, including frontier stories of mountain men and settlers with Shakespeare books in their saddlebags. But it also traces parallel histories—of itinerant actors and actresses, of women's reading groups, of educators and their students, of diverse performances and readings of Shakespeare's works. Looking at the history of Montana from the Shakespearean perspective allows for unusual insights, just as looking at the cultural phenomenon of "Shakespeare" against the backdrop of this geographical place adds to how we understand his global influence. Tracing more than two centuries of history over a huge geographical area results in a vast array of different voices, so it is not possible (or desirable) to provide a neat schematic of what Shakespeare has meant to Montana. Several common threads, however, suggest themselves across these narratives, including:

- a need to tell and retell stories, to participate in the creation of myths about Shakespearean encounters in the West;
- an impulse to *perform* the stories of Shakespeare, both on and off the stage;
- a desire to take ownership of Shakespeare, co-opting his works to speak for the readers' morality and aspirations;
- a heightened awareness of how Shakespeare, the "largest" of authors, can fill the vast and supposedly empty landscapes of Montana;
- a nostalgia for a lost past in which both the frontier and its romantic encounters with Shakespeare have receded.

All of Montana is a stage, allowing for repeated performances that, in the words of ethnographer Norman Denzin, "forge a bond between an imagined past and the present," where "performers stand on both sides of history at the same time."[6] Shakespeare has always been the author, and the symbol, that allowed them to do so.

Shakespeare imagined his country's geography most movingly in John of Gaunt's "sceptered isle" speech in *Richard II*, calling Britain a "fortress built by Nature for herself," a "little world," and a "precious stone set in the silver sea" (2.1.40–46).[7] Shakespeare's evocative landscapes invariably capture his Montana audiences; he not only wrote of islands like Britain, but he imagined

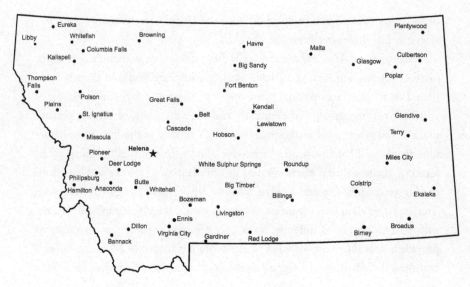

Map 1. Map of Montana.

places in Europe and the New World where he had never set foot. Sometimes, too, the mysteries of an ancient past are conveyed through the land, such as the awesome cliffs of Dover or the hostile barrenness of the heath in *King Lear*. In the American West, the real and imagined landscapes tend toward the open, the vast, the raw and dangerous expanses of the unknown. Those who have read and seen Shakespeare in Montana have been endlessly fascinated by the ways in which his characters negotiate analogous places.

The Shakespearean play that perhaps covers the broadest geographical scope and is infused with the most nostalgia is *Antony and Cleopatra*. Just before Cleopatra's death she speaks of the departed Antony, depicting him as a colossus whose qualities exceeded imagination itself. She alternately upholds this as fiction and insists upon its truth, saying that if there "ever were one such, / It's past the size of dreaming" (5.2.95–96). Shakespeare in Montana unfolds in a way analogous to Cleopatra's memory of Antony: past the size of dreaming.

PROLOGUE

Waiting for the Shakespeare

But look, the morn, in russet mantle clad,
Walks o'er the dew of yon high eastward hill.

—*Hamlet*

In 1980, Joel Jahnke had just taken over as the artistic director of Montana Shakespeare in the Parks (MSIP), an outreach organization of Montana State University that had begun in 1973 with the mission to perform Shakespeare's plays—free and outdoors—to communities across Montana. Already he knew that there was one place everyone always talked about: a performance site in the southeastern part of the state atop a 4,300-foot butte on state forest land, ten miles outside a tiny ranching community called Birney, situated in the Tongue River Valley and a stone's throw from the Northern Cheyenne Indian Reservation. For anyone connected with MSIP, Jahnke's story of his first journey to Poker Jim Butte is legendary:

> I was driving on dirt roads and kept getting further and further away from anything. And then there was that damn sign: *Birney, Montana, Population 17.* I pulled up at the general store and saw two kids sitting by the mailbox. I walked over to them and said hi . . . and then I asked, "What are you doing?" They responded, "We're waiting for the Shakespeare." . . . It's like they were waiting for the circus.

At that moment, Jahnke realized that "this was something bigger than what I thought I would ever do."[1]

Poker Jim Butte is still a stop on the eleven-actor tour, which now performs two plays in repertory for sixty-two communities across Montana and the surrounding states. MSIP is one of Montana's most cherished cultural institutions, for over the course of forty-seven seasons the company has reached three quarters of a million audience members.[2] Many have told, in brief, the rich history of MSIP; it has been featured in the *New York Times*, on *NBC Nightly News*, on PBS's *Backroads of Montana*, and in a 2015 PBS documentary entitled *Bard in the Backcountry*. Every time the company receives news coverage, however, the most prominent focus is always Poker Jim Butte; this location and the legends associated with the performances there have gained mythic status.[3] I have been to the Poker Jim Butte performances many times, and I too am drawn to the allure of the place—its landscape, its community, and the improbable continuation of Shakespeare in the most isolated and underpopulated countryside imaginable.

The residents of Birney and its surrounding areas are proud people. Settlers from the American South and homesteaders from Norway moved into the region in the last two decades of the nineteenth century immediately after the indigenous people were forcibly removed, setting up cattle operations and eventually dude ranches that attracted visitors who wanted a taste of the "authentic" West. Photos from the mid-twentieth century depict a thriving community, boasting not only a post office and general store but the Corell Dance Hall and saloon, where weekly Saturday dances were enormously popular.[4] The vibrancy of this community was palpable, but by the 1970s things had begun to change. As in many rural communities, the population declined as more people moved to cities and never returned; the dance hall and saloon closed, and although the general store was still operating when MSIP started performing in the 1970s, by the '90s it was gone too. Meanwhile, heavy disputes over coal and methane in the area divided the community. By the time that MSIP came to town, this one- or two-evening performance on the butte was the sole annual community event—the only excuse for gathering the far-flung residents of Rosebud County together into a semblance of the community that they once were.

The success of MSIP in Birney has everything to do with one particular family: the Fjells. Butch Fjell had loved Shakespeare since his memorable high school class, so in the second year of the tour, he and his wife Laurel took over the sponsorship required to bring MSIP to a particular community; they organized homestays, collected what money they could to contribute to the company, cooked and coordinated a potluck for actors and audience members after the show. Laurel, the postmistress of Birney, served as the Shakespearean ambassador of the area, organizing a "Turkey Shoot for Shakespeare" fund-raiser and pressing everyone to attend. The energy she and Butch poured into this was well rewarded, for a crowd that was ten times larger than Birney's population regularly attended. The Fjells saw this event as "an extension of the family,"[5] and as such it created a bond not just within their own literal family but far beyond. For Kelsey Walton, Butch and Laurel's granddaughter, MSIP's annual visit was what she solemnly described as "the happiest day of [her] life" when she was little, for the actors absorbed her into the troupe, allowing her to help set up the stage and pass out programs. The day after the performance they observed the tradition of jumping off a bridge to swim in the Tongue River. Kelsey's upbringing is woven together with these performances: she notes that she attended from the time when she "came out of the womb" and always understood the language, as if it were her original tongue; she sat enrapt by the performances, dreaming of becoming a player.[6] While other residents of Birney had much more concrete views of the event, they have nonetheless benefited from the dreamer that Kelsey became. In 2015, after her grandparents retired from the sponsorship and a local wealthy donor had moved away, there was doubt that MSIP would come to Poker Jim.[7] Desperate not to let the tradition die, Kelsey (aged eighteen) did a full fund-raising campaign, gathering enough money to sponsor the show—with some left over for 2016. Asked why it was so important to carry on the tradition, she said, "It's such a big cultural event, and not having it in Birney would be like the sun not coming up."[8]

The lure of geography is central to understanding what it is like to perform, and witness, Shakespeare atop Poker Jim Butte. Southeastern Montana presents a lonesome landscape, much less majestic than the mountains in the western part of the state. In one sense, the landscape looks flat, giving full perspective to why people refer to the area as "the big sky." Yet the topography is full of vertical features that made the Tongue River Valley a safe haven for Crow and Lakota peoples and fertile land for bison and cattle. Poker Jim Butte stands dramatically over this entire area, providing the most commanding view. The landscape is best described by the cowboy poet Wallace McRae:

Only the curvature of the Earth prevents one from seeing—as Henry Bailey once responded to the question of how far you can see from the top of that hill—"all the way to St. Paul." The Wolf Mountains, blue as a morning glory, are to the west. South of them, father away, fainter but higher, are the Big Horns. And the rest of the compass points feature ponderosa, prairie, plains and mesas in a jumble of shapes, sizes and shades and varying hues, from the warm yellows of sandstone, the hot magenta and rose of the scoria and clinker divide tops, cooling to the greens of grass, juniper, and pines and finally the misty blues of distance and sky that blend together until there is no clearly defined horizon.[9]

The awesome natural beauty of the butte is accompanied by elements that invariably make performing outdoors a challenge. Film star Bill Pullman began his acting career with MSIP, and he reflected upon how "there's nothing more magical than having the elements around you," especially when you look out from Poker Jim Butte to see the multiple weather fronts moving in, "so you have that kind of excitement of being outdoors and feeling there's some wind coming on and maybe we're gonna have to make some changes if the rain front comes."[10] Only twice did MSIP need to cancel the performance on the butte, despite years of extreme heat, lightning storms, wind that almost blew the stage over, and sudden sheets of rain.

In 1937, an article from the *Billings Gazette* reported that a newly built structure in Custer National Forest—the fire lookout tower on Poker Jim Butte—had been attracting dozens of tourists from the local dude ranch who climbed the lookout tower in order to view the countryside from the best vantage point.[11] The butte became a popular site for picnics and sightseeing, while the lookout tower provided an invaluable aid for spotting fires in the surrounding forests. Satellite-enabled technology has made most fire lookouts obsolete, but the Poker Jim lookout is one of only two that still operate in Montana today. Every summer, the fire ranger knows what will happen on one evening in July: a troupe of ten or eleven actors will drive up the butte in two trucks and a trailer, set up a stage, and be joined by over a hundred people who come from a hundred mile radius to watch an evening Shakespeare performance as the sun goes down. The ranger becomes accustomed to giving tours of his tower and his one-room home atop it while the sweaty actors prepare for the show and slip into costumes. Sometimes fire crews from the

Figure 1. The glow of the picnic shelter, where the MSIP actors are served dinner after their performance, is dwarfed by the lightning storm over Poker Jim Butte. Photo by Andrew Rathgeber, 2019.

region will take the opportunity to catch the performance as well. Michael Richards, a United States Forest Service firefighter who attended once, admitted that the main reason the crew piled into the truck to watch a play was because it was "a social and cultural event of a unique nature for rural eastern Montana"—one that could provide the much-desired company of women and booze without needing to drive two hours to Sheridan or Miles City.[12] Perhaps this is not what Butch and Laurel dreamed of when they called this tradition their "one shot at culture"[13] in Birney, but no matter what the spectators are looking for, they tend to find it in the curious mixture of people on a summer evening each year.

To view the landscape from the top of the butte means to look in vain for population centers. Most striking, in fact, is how the land betrays so few signs of modern civilization. Actors remark on the beauty of the landscape, but they also balk at the bizarre notion that an audience would emerge from such an empty place—people who want to sit on the grass in the heat of a summer

Figure 2. The view from the Poker Jim Butte fire tower. Photo by Kevin Brustuen, 2019.

evening to watch Shakespeare. Rhonda Smith, who first toured in 1975, described the moment of "looking out and seeing the dust come off the gravel roads" as the audience members began to appear, as if out of nowhere.[14] The same phenomenon struck Joel Jahnke forcefully during his first visit in 1980: "I went to the top of this damn Butte, and it was just stunning. . . . I asked [the actor] Tom Morris, 'Who the hell would come up here to see Shakespeare?' 'Just wait,' said Tom. Then I started seeing the dust from the pickups. Truck after truck—probably 140 people."[15] No matter how often this phenomenon is described, it always takes on an air of the mystical. Will Dickerson, former actor and occasional director of MSIP's plays, describes the event in this way: "It's like Laurel and Butch are the high priest and priestess who conjure the people" on the butte to witness the ritual of drama, sunset, and festival.[16]

From its earliest days, MSIP has maintained the same mission: to bring quality, live theatrical productions of Shakespeare and other classics to communities in Montana and surrounding states, with an emphasis on underserved, rural areas who would not otherwise have this opportunity.[17] Liz

Reierson is one resident of Montana who epitomizes what it means to come from an underserved, rural area. Every year her mother and grandmother forced the family (including multiple cousins) to go to Poker Jim when she was a teenager, even though they came from far outside the Birney circuit (some seventy-five miles to the east). In addition to being tired from the long drive on dirt roads in 2005, Reierson was disappointed to see that MSIP would be performing a play she had never heard of: *Cymbeline*. Her description of that performance, though, leaves little doubt about the mark it made on her:

> At the point where Imogen wakes and believes her love was slaughtered beside her, the young blonde playing Imogen let out a cry that shook the whole crowd. It was gut wrenching, and painful. In that moment, her pain was my pain. The play would continue, and eventually the ending in which all the wrongs are righted would be made complete as the sun began to set. The purples and pinks softly framed the family and the stage as the play drew to a close. The stage would be taken down by the audience as well as the actors and we finished the day by eating a light picnic with the players.[18]

Reierson's memory of the play melts into a description of the landscape, audience, and company—a sentiment shared by so many who have been there.[19]

Reierson went on to become a high school teacher in eastern Montana, but her devotion to rural education is by no means an anomaly. The rugged individualism of Birney ranchers runs parallel to a strong emphasis upon self-betterment and education in rural Montana, which is an attitude that has in large part allowed MSIP to flourish. Thus, in the early years many of the communities that sponsored MSIP were led by older women—the same ones who ran reading groups and formed chapters of the League of Women Voters. Arts events were fundamental to the kind of community they wanted to build, but while the women took on the task of organizing, they managed to draw an impressive cross-section of the community to the performances. Pictures of past performances at Poker Jim Butte tell a striking story of the constituency: cowboys standing in the back wearing their Wranglers and hats, hippies sporting long hair and bandanas, Native Americans from the nearby Northern Cheyenne Indian Reservation standing in the back, children splayed on picnic

Figure 3. Audience members watch a performance on Poker Jim Butte during the first MSIP complete season in 1974. Photo courtesy of MSIP archives.

blankets, young couples sipping from cans of beer. The community is also marked by a diversity of economic status: those with very little extra money and those owning multimillion-dollar ranches. This was exactly what MSIP founder Bruce Jacobsen had envisioned as appropriate to this tour, which draws "people of all walks of life, all ages" who enjoy Shakespeare, because "Shakespeare wrote for that kind of an audience, a cross-section of society."[20]

At its best, this instantiation of live, outdoor theatre gives rise to a collaboration between actors and audience. Actors who have performed on the butte invariably say that this audience contains astute critics whose responses have made them into better artists with a deeper sense of what they do. Kevin Asselin, who has been the artistic director of MSIP since 2014, tells the story of performing in 2003, when a wizened cowboy approached him after the show, pulled out his tattered copy of *As You Like It*, and said that he thought Shakespeare had tremendous wisdom in depicting Duke Senior's court in the woods.[21] Even more than the expected clichés about Shakespeare's portrayal of the wilderness, however, the actors notice this audience's facility with the language and their appreciation of directorial decisions. Jahnke recalls a time when he was talking with Butch and another local after a performance of *Twelfth Night*, and they began comparing this actor's approach to Malvolio to one they had seen seven years before: "It was bizarre to have a conversation like this, up here, with these people," said Jahnke. "Over time I began to realize that we had this little pocket of sophisticated people who had seen more Shakespeare than 99 percent of New Yorkers. We had helped train them. What an interesting road that was for me, to see the sophistication of the company and of our audiences at the same time. They are very discerning."[22]

Despite such stories that attest to an engagement with the drama itself, it is also clear that Shakespeare is in some sense ancillary to the creation of community atop the butte every July. Morris and Jahnke both describe MSIP as a rough equivalent of the circus—the main attraction in a rural community, providing much-needed entertainment. For some viewers, the landscape and the art remain in an uneasy relationship to one another. Thus Wallace McRae, who came to see a production of *Love's Labour's Lost* in 1997, noted that the audience seemed "distracted from the magnificence of Shakespearean words, phrases and rhyme by our ethereal surroundings. Our eyes are drawn from the stage and the actors to the vastness of panoramic views, and our cultural trappings are almost intrusive in this wild and beautiful place." McRae concluded that the performance was in fact "diminished by the setting" and wondered why the actors loved performing on Poker Jim, where they are "upstaged by the pastoral panoramic setting."[23] Even when he attended the dance and dinner hosted by the Fjells later that night, McRae couldn't help but view these actors, hailing from cities in eastern states, as outsiders reminiscent of the tourists to the Birney dude ranches in the mid-twentieth century.[24] What McRae didn't know, however, is the deep sense of integration that the actors have felt with the Birney community since the earliest touring days of MSIP.

When Bruce Jacobsen booked the first tour, he chose Birney because his mother lived there. Family, in fact, is the foundation of the community, thus Laurel characterizes MSIP as "an extension of the family."[25] Tom Morris reflects that in his fourteen years of touring with the company, he got to know the members of the community, watched the kids grow up, and even felt deeply moved by seeing their tragedies—especially the car accident that killed Butch and Laurel Fjell's son Elmer in 2001. After that, says Morris, "you could feel the emptiness."[26] From the beginning, the Fjells established the close connection with the company; as Rhonda Smith says, they were simply "down home people," and the homestays further developed the sense of community.[27] Even in the beginning of the twenty-first century, the profound sense of belonging to the community made the experience magical to actor Matt Foss, who characterized Birney as the epitome of the eastern Montana portion of the tour, for it taught him about family and hospitality. He chose homestays where he could help do chores and try to imagine himself as a permanent member of the household. Joel and Kathy Jahnke became deeply committed to the Fjells, sharing meals, Christmas gifts, and car-repair emergencies. The sense that the Fjells and their community are family spreads to the actors, who come to the tour, even as novices, understanding that they are about to be part of something larger—a particular clan centered upon this mythic place with the mythic names: Poker Jim, Hanging Woman Creek, the Tongue River.

Foss, who is now a professor of theatre in Ohio, looks back on his performances in Birney as the main inspiration for his continuing mission to do free theatre:

> The relationship I seek to foster with the stories we create and the audiences we find looks like what you see on top of the butte. You can see Butch standing in the back, Laurel in her big sun hat, Kelsey running around, and everybody's line of cars, like the end of *Field of Dreams*, snaking up the road.[28]

For many who have observed this phenomenon, "If you build it, they will come"[29] has seemed an appropriate way to describe the magic of theatre in southeastern Montana, emerging from the visions of Jacobsen and Jahnke, and overseen by the dedication of the Fjells, their families, and neighbors.

Times have undoubtedly changed: now actors camp rather than having homestays that connect them intimately with the community, now Birney doesn't have any stores, now Kelsey has moved away, and Butch and Laurel do not even attend every year. In 2018 Cindy Hagen, who is married to a fifth-generation Montanan from that area, took over the sponsorship. She raises money through GoFundMe campaigns and provides three meals for the actors during their sojourn to an area that is, Hagen points out, "not just rural, but remote—one of the most remote places in the lower forty-eight states."

Figure 4. My son, Luke, watches the MSIP actors put up the stage atop Poker Jim Butte. Photo by the author, 2014.

For a while it seemed that the tradition of MSIP on Poker Jim might be dwindling, but new families with young children have started to make the trek up to the butte, and Hagen is determined to use crowdsourcing as an advantage so that the community feels invested in this event.[30]

What keeps the place most alive, though, is the stories themselves, which create a nostalgia that gives rise to myth. The repetition of the anecdotes, like the ritual of return to Poker Jim, is an essential component of the creation of this place.[31] As Will Dickerson articulates it, the ritual of this event testifies to a community's need to embrace the transcendence of Shakespearean storytelling. McRae wondered whether those watching a Shakespeare performance on the butte were on a sort of vision quest. Others might call it a pilgrimage, but the impulse to use religious language is constant. The profound links between this site, history, and ritual demonstrate the ways in which "place, or the cultural landscape, is quietly alive with memories—other people's memories."[32] The need to be part of the community atop this butte pulls at me, as it has pulled at many before. I thus add my voice, and my memories, to the fabric of storytelling that has created a mythical place called Poker Jim Butte—not the precise geographical location, but the community event that was generated by a surprising need to witness Shakespeare once a year.

The story of Poker Jim Butte epitomizes the relationship that Montana has had with Shakespeare. This relationship is characterized by unlikely encounters in vast landscapes, by legends that circulate far beyond the events that inspire them, and by nostalgia for a time that has receded, yet is still almost within reach. In one of Shakespeare's most nostalgic tragedies, *Antony and Cleopatra*, the soldier Enobarbus reflects upon what it means to inhabit a crucial period in history and thus to "earn a place i'th' story."[33] In order to understand how and why Shakespeare has consistently earned his own place in the history of Montana, we must go back to a time before this region had such a name—a time when it was part of a huge land sale called the Louisiana Purchase.

MEN OF THE MOUNTAINS

We'll higher to the mountains; there secure us.

—*Cymbeline*

When the men of Lewis and Clark's expedition, the Corps of Discovery, first journeyed through what is now Montana in 1805, their days were filled with the difficult work of finding their way up the Missouri River and trying to understand a land that was a mystery to nonindigenous peoples. Thomas Jefferson had charged them with the task of charting this huge land that the United States had bought from France—an expanse of 827,000 square miles about which they knew next to nothing. Today Montana's roads are dotted with interpretive signs, marking spots on the Lewis and Clark Trail; the history of this region always seems to return to this restless and active group of men, for the Lewis and Clark expedition has come to represent the grandeur of the place as the white men first saw and mapped it.

Rocky Mountain College

Encouraged by what the Corps of Discovery learned about the land's natural resources, mountain men came westward in the ensuing decades, looking for wealth and opportunity. These men faced dangers and traveled extensively, but this life also required patience through long periods of idleness. Trapper

Osborne Russell spoke of winters not far from modern-day Red Lodge, Montana, when he and his men "had nothing to do but to eat, attend to the horses and procure fire wood," so they spent their time reading.[1] The books they carried with them and used as their constant companions included works by Lord Byron, Sir Walter Scott, Shakespeare, and the Bible. Reading was not just a solitary pastime, however, but a way to forge a community among the outspoken and often learned mountain men. A nostalgic Russell recalled of times that went back as early as 1824:

> We all had snug lodges made of dressed Buffaloe skins in the center of which we built a fire. . . . The long winter evenings were passed away by collecting in some of the most spacious lodges and entering into debates arguments or spinning long yarns until midnight in perfect good humour and I for one will cheerfully confess that I have derived no little benefit from the frequent arguments and debates held in what we termed The Rocky Mountain College and I doubt not but some of my comrades who considered themselves Classical Scholars have had some little added to their wisdom in these assemblies however rude they might appear.[2]

Russell spoke fondly of the power of stories—especially those derived from Shakespeare—on those long winter nights. The men circulated the books they possessed and then took to "spinning long yarns" of their own.

Russell's 1835 expedition included a trapper named Joe Meek. This young, uneducated mountain man listened eagerly to his fellow trappers and learned a great deal in this makeshift "Rocky Mountain College." Meek's biographer, Frances Victor, writes:

> Some of the better educated men, who had once known and loved books, but whom some mishap in life had banished to the wilderness, recalled their favorite authors, and recited passages once treasured, now growing unfamiliar; or whispered to some chosen confrere the saddened history of his earlier years.[3]

The recitation of stories and passages from literature was common among explorers, who relied upon the spoken word as a means of information, education, and moral direction. It was also a vital way to keep one's spirits up. The

first anecdote about any sort of performance in the greater Yellowstone region comes from Alexander Ross's trapping expedition in 1824. Ross found
that his men had become "discouraged, despondent and gloomy," so in order
to dispel this mood, he enlisted the help of a fiddle player in the party and put
together an evening show in the tent. Everyone was asked to become part of
the entertainment, presenting a song, dance, story, or recitation. The revelry
continued into the night, and Ross reported that "the morning found the
gloom entirely dispelled, and with everyone in a good humor, the men went
back to their gigantic task in earnest."[4]

Such amateur theatrics were no doubt a vital part of evenings around
campfires. Yet theatrical and literary endeavors were not only about entertainment and dispelling the gloom, for they also served as a medium of highly
valued knowledge. "It will not be thought discreditable to our young trapper,"
the biographer writes of Joe Meek, "that he learned to read by the light of the
campfire. Becoming sensible, even in the wilderness, of the deficiencies of his
early education, he found a teacher in a comrade . . . and soon acquired sufficient knowledge to enjoy an old copy of Shakespeare, which, with a Bible, was
carried about with the property of the camp."[5] Numerous anecdotes place
Shakespeare alongside the Bible in this manner, for these were assumed to be
the most significant works of Western culture. That people from all walks of
American life acknowledged Shakespeare's importance is clear. It is in this
spirit that the French diplomat Alexis de Tocqueville famously remarked that
when he toured America in 1831 he was surprised to find that "there is hardly
a pioneer's hut which does not contain a few odd volumes of Shakespeare."[6]
Surprisingly, however, early nineteenth-century educational curricula in the
United States did not as a rule include Shakespeare, so learning to read with
and by Shakespeare was an enterprise unique to autodidacts such as the
mountain men.[7] And though the precise nature of the relationship between
these explorers and the early modern playwright is lost to us, stories like the
one about Meek show how hungry some of these men were not just to pos-
sess the Shakespearean books but to fully understand them.

While we might assume that the practical knowledge required for men
such as Russell and Meek to survive and prosper in the wilderness was worlds
removed from sixteenth- and seventeenth-century literature, these men clearly
saw it differently. The frontiersman and trapper W. T. Hamilton, for instance,
was adamant about the importance of classic literature; he and his companions

in the West were all great readers, devouring books on ancient history along-side Shakespeare. Hamilton wryly commented that "it was always amusing to me to hear people from the East speak of old mountaineers as semi-barbarians, when as a general rule they were the peers of the Easterners in general knowledge."[8] Hamilton's pride about these learned mountaineers was accompanied by a desire to let other people know about them, and he was not alone in this desire. As a result, these bookish men became the subjects of further yarns about the frontier.

By far the most common stories about Shakespeare in the Northern Rockies revolve around the colorful mountain man, trapper, army scout, and wilderness guide Jim Bridger. Multiple versions of Bridger's love of and encounters with Shakespeare survive from nineteenth-century accounts, providing an array of fascinating anecdotes, some of which may indeed be tall tales. The obsessive interest in these anecdotes is itself a crucial part of understanding Shakespeare in the West. Such stories about Bridger began to circulate in print as early as 1864, and no doubt they had a rich oral history preceding this. They paint a vivid picture of a grizzled, illiterate, outspoken mountain man who had a love for Shakespeare's stories and language. Numerous witnesses were fascinated by the seeming incongruity between Bridger as an uncouth, uneducated trail guide and the notion of Shakespeare as an arbiter of classical, genteel culture.

The narratives agree that Bridger became intent upon owning a Shakespeare book, giving various accounts of how he acquired it—usually from a passing wagon train, or from emigrants on the Oregon Trail, in exchange for a valuable yoke of oxen. All versions of the story take time to portray an intensely interested Bridger who must rely on an intermediary who can read the words to him. Some say this was a fellow soldier, a hired hand, a German boy, or even, most intriguingly, the Irish nobleman Sir St. George Gore, for whom Bridger served as a guide during his years hunting big game in the West.[9] The aural component of these stories is crucial, for Bridger is depicted listening carefully, spellbound for a time, until he explodes with a negative reaction to what he hears. He apparently had a tendency to criticize the morals of Shakespeare's characters. Speaking of the usually beloved character Sir John Falstaff, Bridger said that "that thar big Dutchman, Mr. Full-stuff," was "a leetle bit too fond of lager beer" and suggested that "it might have been better for the old man" if he had instead stuck to "good old Bourbon whisky."[10] A stronger reaction accompanied Bridger's outrage at the moment

Figure 5. Jim Bridger, the illiterate mountain man who loved Shakespeare, circa 1859–1875. MHS Legacy Photograph Collection, 941-200. Montana Historical Society Research Center archives.

in *Richard III* when the tyrant king orders the murders of the princes in the Tower of London. Bridger, according to many sources, threw the book into the fire upon hearing this part of the story; in another version, he brandished his gun, vowing to kill Richard. One officer's wife reported that Bridger exclaimed that "Shakspeare must have had a bad heart and been as [damned] mean as a Sioux, to have written such scoundrolism as that."[11] Was this the end of a short-lived love affair that Bridger had with Shakespeare? Most stories say yes, but J. Lee Humfreville's compelling recollection was that for years afterward, "it was amusing to hear Bridger quote Shakespeare. He could give quotation after quotation, and was always ready to do so. Sometimes he seasoned them with a broad oath, so ingeniously inserted as to make it appear to the listener that Shakespeare himself had used the same language."[12] This description of Bridger's hybrid speech points to a key similarity between the illiterate mountain man and the playwright from rural England: they both relished the use of memorable turns of phrase, creative metaphors, and language that could fully express the range of human emotions.

Those who recount such stories strive to answer the question of how Bridger would have known about Shakespeare at all. In addition to conjectures about army mates or Sir St. George Gore as the purveyor of information, one source claims that Bridger went to New York City himself and saw a performance of *A Midsummer Night's Dream* (an extraordinarily unlikely scenario), while others aver that he saw Shakespearean performances at Fort Laramie (which is possible). However, decades before Gore and before these colorful accounts of Bridger were written, this mountain man was a companion of Osborne Russell and Joe Meek, and thus was undoubtedly exposed to the informal "Rocky Mountain College." This often-overlooked information suggests that Bridger's original encounters with Shakespeare were probably not so momentous and colorful as the stories written about him after the fact claim. In other words, Bridger probably held a copy of Shakespeare much earlier, and perhaps much more frequently, than these funny stories assert.

As Russell's account makes clear, long intervals between tasks, especially during winter encampments, made books prized possessions. The first newspaper in Montana was not established until 1864, so until that time reading material was limited to the books that the mountain men and settlers carried with them. But carry them they did. The wagon trains, as attested by the Bridger anecdotes, could be counted on to have books. The theory that Bridger, after hearing Shakespeare's collected works was the best book that had ever been written, "made a journey to the main road, and lay in wait for a wagon train, and bought a copy from some emigrants" is not implausible, because copies of Shakespeare were often transported by the settlers.[13] Nonetheless, Bridger's quest for the Shakespeare volume is another logical leap in the legendary history, because Fort Laramie itself had a library of six hundred books; thus Bridger need not have bargained with emigrants to get his hands on a copy of Shakespeare's plays.[14]

Yet once again, the anecdotes point to some deeper truths about what it meant for a legend like Bridger to desire the knowledge contained within Shakespeare. One strand of the story narrates an extensive dialogue in which Bridger enters into some hard bargaining with a traveler who wants to buy a yoke of oxen, but Bridger refuses until he realizes that this man possesses a copy of Shakespeare. Once he is assured that this is, in fact, a "genuine Shakespeare book," Bridger is content to trade the oxen for the tome. Such a trade means that he was paying $150–200 for the Shakespeare collection. The enormous price (even if apocryphal) points to the value of the book—a value determined not by its practical usage on the frontier or its market price, but by a belief that it contained something more intangible that Bridger sought. Was it wisdom? Poetry? Insight into history? Or perhaps simply arresting tales that captured his imagination? It could have been any or all of these reasons, but because Bridger never wrote an account of his own life, our view of his relationship to Shakespeare is mediated by second- and third-hand observers. The story of Shakespeare in Montana is built of anecdotes like this one, circulating in multiple copies and not always verifiable by the historical record. Yet the tales that people choose to tell are themselves a testimony to how consistently people on this huge frontier reached for Shakespeare's words, works, and characters.

Precious Books

Unlike Bridger, the pioneer Granville Stuart *did* write his own story about his experiences, eventually publishing his reminiscences in a work entitled *Forty Years on the Frontier*. Stuart loved to read, so one of his struggles during his years in the Northern Rockies was finding enough material. In 1860 he and his brother James made what Granville recorded as a sort of heroic journey in order to acquire precious books. He wrote that "James and I were both great readers and we had been all winter without so much as an almanac to look at," so "we were famished for something to read." When they heard from some Native peoples that there was a man in the Bitterroot Valley with a trunk full of books, the brothers immediately "saddled our horses and putting our blankets, and some dried meat for food, on a pack horse, we started for those books, a hundred and fifty miles away, without a house, or anybody on the route, and with three big dangerous rivers to cross." The journey was not a disappointment: "How we feasted our eyes on those books. We could hardly make up our minds which ones to choose." They settled on five volumes, at $5 apiece, including illustrated copies of Shakespeare and Byron, and though they had little money left, "we had the blessed books, which we packed carefully in our blankets, and joyfully started on our return ride of a hundred and fifty miles."[15] Stuart's flowery first-person narrative of this event underlines a genuine passion for these handsome copies of British works. The Shakespeare book was undoubtedly one of the illustrated volumes by Charles Knight, a

Figure 6. Granville Stuart, who rode 150 miles on horseback in 1860 to acquire five books, including an illustrated copy of Shakespeare's works. Photo by L. A. Huffman, 1883. Catalog number 981-260. Montana Historical Society Research Center archives.

popular edition of the plays that was made possible by the mass production of wood-engraved illustrations. That such books, created and published in London in the 1840s, were in the Bitterroot Valley in 1860 shows just how far and wide Shakespeare traveled, appreciated by denizens of the most remote landscapes.

Granville Stuart's accounts of his explorations around Montana, especially in the Deer Lodge Valley, abound with observations about the land, sketches of what he saw, and accounts of what he took with him. His impressions are framed by his references to Shakespeare, such as when he complains that too many of the territorial governors come from New England, thus they are not "native, and to the manner born."[16] This quotation from *Hamlet* is not at all central to the play but is merely a passing reference about distasteful Danish customs, so it is all the more striking that Stuart comfortably employs it when considering the differences between politicians from the East and from

Montana territory. He took ownership of Shakespeare's words in the same way that he took a fierce pride in separating outsiders from native inhabitants of Montana.

In 1866 Stuart visited St. Louis, but he disliked the city immensely. Attending his first performances of Shakespeare, he saw the acclaimed actor Edwin Forrest play King Lear, as well as the popular role of Cardinal Richelieu in a play by Edward Bulwer-Lytton. Stuart wrote that he "didn't like Forrest's blood-and-thunder acting; he tears a passion all to tatters," and the production of *Hamlet* he saw did not equal his expectations.[17] Stuart always felt more at home in Montana, and, along with his sense of belonging, he had strong opinions about what Shakespeare meant and, consequently, how his plays should be staged. His reviews of the plays point to a desire for authenticity and an honest portrayal of character that did not rely on excessive displays of emotion. It was with this same restraint that he presented himself in his role as a frontiersman.

Stuart, who was sometimes known by the moniker "Mr. Montana," tried his hand at many occupations; he was by turns a cattleman, merchant, gold prospector, and historian. His diverse experiences echo the versatility and volatility of the frontier days. It is striking that when he published his *Forty Years on the Frontier* in 1926, the perceived wildness and remoteness of the West seemed so recent. The *New York Times* reviewer of Stuart's book wrote that "lovers of frontier lore should be grateful for the salvaging of so many tales of high emprise which deserve a place in the folklore of America."[18] The Stuart brothers' journey to acquire copies of Shakespeare and Byron is precisely the kind of story that readers from the eastern United States loved to see, for it spoke to fantasies that were by equal turns familiar and tantalizingly alien.

Martialing Shakespeare

Like Stuart, the military men dispatched to Montana Territory were often well-educated and in search of any sign of culture during their stints in the West. In the 1870s, the United States army increased its presence in Montana because of building tensions with the Sioux. John Bourke, a captain who served under General George Crook during this period, characterized himself and others in the company as frequent readers—a pastime in which the soldiers indulged during long periods of waiting for orders, as long as reading material could be found. Bourke explained that "newspapers were read to pieces, and such books as had found their way with the command were passed from hand to hand and read eagerly."[19] He and some of the other men agreed that each day they would peruse either a Shakespearean play or else an essay by the Whig historian Thomas Macaulay, then discuss them together. Given Macaulay's view of England's place as a civilizing force, the interest that these military men had in his essays must have been driven by their own mission to deal with the "Indian problem" in the American West. Reading Macaulay next to Shakespeare's history plays—which have often been viewed as a celebration of Tudor power—probably allowed for a positive interpretation of the role of providence and violence in European civilization's forward movement.

Many commanding officers brought a love of Shakespeare with them from the East, where they were educated. West Point Academy in particular took pride in its inclusion of a classical curriculum that helped to martial its men's minds in the service of a godly mission to defend the United States, especially in the years following the Civil War. Shakespeare was a vital component of such education, and the officers certainly knew and appreciated his plays, especially the histories and Roman tragedies. On the lighter side, the West Point men frequently wrote and performed in entertainments such as "Sheelshakes" and "Ye Soul Stirring Tragedy," Shakespearean knock-off comedies with music. Some of these playlets were created by Fayette W. Roe, a United States Army officer who was later stationed at Fort Shaw in the northern part of Montana and who presided over the regimental band.[20] Music, theatre, and reading worked together to provide entertainment in the military forts. Shakespeare's works, too, came from West Point to the real West as part of the project to civilize through military control.

Another West Point graduate, George Armstrong Custer, derived from his education a deep appreciation for drama, so he attended the theatre in New York regularly. Custer also had a flair for drama in his personal life, and like a character in a play, he transformed himself repeatedly. By sitting for portraits, dressing as a frontiersman, and presenting himself through speech and written language, he constructed a persona to suit his ambitions. He formed a close friendship with the notable Shakespearean actor Lawrence Barrett, who played frequently alongside Edwin Booth. Custer's appropriation of Shakespearean stories was thorough; in a recent biography T. J. Stiles even wonders whether Custer deliberately modeled himself after Henry V.[21] It would make sense that Custer was leaning on this Shakespearean source as the inspiration for his planned reformation: from the rowdy youngster who was court-martialed during his time at West Point to the glorious general of the 7th Cavalry. Like the famous frontier showman Buffalo Bill, Custer used the elusive and romantic idea of the West to act in a script that he desperately sought to author. He donned the costume of the frontiersman, fully inhabiting the mountain man persona, carrying on a George Gore–like urge to subdue the wilderness. But history does not always cooperate with the commander's fantasies. Henry V *did* win the battle of Agincourt, but Custer was defeated at Little Bighorn.

Following this defeat in 1876, the United States military launched a renewed campaign for the men stationed on the frontier to vanquish their indigenous opponents and to uphold the rectitude of Western morals and ideals. Fort Keogh (near Miles City) was built two months after the Battle of Little Bighorn in order to serve as a base so that the Sioux and Cheyenne could be contained and prevented from escaping to Canada.[22] Such an assignment also included periods during which the army recruits needed to stave off boredom, so the men looked for distractions that would help them to pass the long stretches of time. Much to the men's delight, in 1889 the Czech-born actress Fanny Janauschek came to Fort Keogh to star in a production of *Macbeth* that promised original music and magnificent costuming. This must have been a particular moment of excitement for the men, for they showed a consistent interest in the theatre. The Fort Keogh Dramatic Company, which performed *Macbeth*, *As You Like It*, and *Julius Caesar*, had been popular for several years with audiences both inside and outside of the fort.[23] Shakespearean performances were likewise part of the culture at other forts across Montana; in addition to providing sources of entertainment, such occasions were windows into stories about warriors in other lands and during other historical moments.

By the end of the nineteenth century, Montana no longer seemed like a wild land, and the explorers and mountain men were largely replaced by entrepreneurs and politicians, many of whom had a military background. In 1889 Montana became a state, and a few years later its chief justice, Decius Wade, made a speech on the courthouse square in Helena. The occasion for his oration was an infantry band performance, so Wade praised the musicians, saying that they were part of a mission to exalt humanity and give them happiness through aesthetic pleasure. Quoting from *Merchant of Venice*, Wade assured his audience that "all the world loves music, except Shakespear's [*sic*] man whose soul was filled with treason, stratagem and spoils." So impressive was the performance of the Third Infantry Band, according to Wade, that it could have even converted such a man who "hath no music in himself."[24] Once again, Shakespeare was seen as a force of civilization, traveling alongside the proud order of the United States military, a champion of regimental order and human dignity promising a great future.

The Vanishing Frontier

For those with more introspective attitudes, this period was a time not just to look forward to the next century in the name of progress but to look back nearly a hundred years to consider the history of this land and its people. In 1893 Granville Stuart was retracing the steps of the Lewis and Clark expedition in the area between the Big Blackfoot River and Flathead Lake. While he commemorated the men who opened up this land for settlers like himself who came after, Stuart also had leisure time, so he brought along a small volume of Shakespeare's plays and strained to read *The Taming of the Shrew* next to the dim firelight of his camp.[25] Did the men of the Corps of Discovery also read Shakespeare on this land at the beginning of the nineteenth century? They would not have done so literally; the weight of essential supplies did not allow for the carrying of books. And yet Shakespeare was certainly carried within the minds of these white explorers. Both Lewis and Clark were familiar with his works, either through education or association with others, perhaps notably Jefferson himself. When John Adams and Thomas Jefferson visited Stratford-upon-Avon in 1786, Jefferson "got on his knees to kiss the ground" in a nearly idolatrous appreciation of Shakespeare.[26]

Two years after the Corps of Discovery expedition, Clark married Julia Hancock, and Lewis gave the couple the complete works of Shakespeare for a wedding present.[27] The Clarks began attending theatre regularly shortly after their wedding and were often audience members at Shakespearean performances. Sacajawea's son Jean Baptiste Charbonneau (nicknamed "Pompey" and often called "Pomp") lived with them in St. Louis and was educated at the Jesuit school there. His education included English, Latin, and Greek; he loved Shakespeare and was also a talented violinist. At the same time, Pomp told stories about his unconventional education on the Corps of Discovery expedition, boasting that he was "born in a canoe." These diverse experiences made Pomp, at least in popular imagination, a thoroughly hybrid man who was as much at home in the wilderness as he was in the cities.[28] According to reports, "anyone who met [Pomp] never forgot the Shakespeare-quoting half-Indian trapper."[29]

Like his parents, Captain William Clark and Julia Hancock, William Preston Clark was fond of attending theatre, and he even acted in Shakespearean plays as a young man. The celebrated painter George Catlin painted a miniature portrait of William as Iago in 1831—a role that he probably played in Philadelphia. Catlin was the consummate Western American artist, famous for his depictions of the Old West and the indigenous peoples of the Plains. From 1845 to 1848 he sponsored a popular tour of the Chippewa Chief Maungwudaus and his entourage to Britain, where they gave entertainments involving both hymn-singing and dancing in "full native costume." This tour included a pilgrimage to Stratford-upon-Avon, where the chief and four members of his troupe signed the register at Shakespeare's Birthplace.[30] Maungwudaus wrote a verse memorial about what it meant to stand where Shakespeare was buried, including the couplet "Rest thou great man under these stones / For there is life yet in thy bones." Even as this Chippewa chief wrote these words, the life of Shakespeare's bones was already extending far into the American West, touching Montana's men, from trappers to settlers, from frontier guides to military generals.

INTERLUDE 1
COWBOYS

That is another simple sin in you:
to bring the ewes and the rams together and to offer
to get your living by the copulation of cattle.

—*As You Like It*

In *As You Like It*, Shakespeare includes a scene in which the clown Touchstone ruminates on the "shepherd's life," in contrast to the life at court. The play's scenes are likewise split between the court and the country, with a clear message that the latter is far preferable. The exiled Duke Senior thus reflects upon the pure state of nature in lines that are probably the most often quoted in reflections upon Shakespeare in the American West:

> Now, my co-mates and brothers in exile,
> Hath not old custom made this life more sweet
> Than that of painted pomp? Are not these woods
> More free from peril than the envious court? . . .
> And this our life, exempt from public haunt,
> Finds tongues in trees, books in the running brooks,
> Sermons in stones, and good in everything. (2.1.1–4, 15–17)

Like the rancher who spoke about this passage at Poker Jim Butte (see prologue), those who have ranged across Montana with their cattle have found

that Duke Senior's words speak to their own experiences and values. By the
end of the nineteenth century, Montana had a sizable population of cowboys;
their lifestyle had a longstanding influence on how people imagined Montana
and continue to do so today.

The romantic image of cowpunchers in the western landscape doesn't always include reading activities, but perhaps it should. Owen Wister's *The Virginian*, published in 1902, is often credited with being the first western ever
written. The titular Virginian, who works as a ranch hand in Wyoming Territory, knows a thing or two about Shakespeare. In one episode, he evokes
"Shakespeare's fat man" (Falstaff), approving of how the playwright "makes
men talk the way they do in life" and musing that Sir John Falstaff would in
fact have made an excellent card player.[1] At another point, the Virginian
speaks about the relative masculine merits of Shakespeare's characters, arguing
that *Romeo and Juliet* has beautiful language, but "Romeo is no man," so he
prefers Mercutio as the real man: "If he had got Juliet there would have been
no foolishness and trouble."[2] As these passages suggest, there was widespread
interest in (not to mention opinions about) Shakespeare among the early
cowboys. Realizing the economic potential of these readers, tobacco manu-
facturers who marketed their products in the late nineteenth century inserted
coupons for books in the pouches they sold, enabling cowboys to procure
miniature abridged volumes of Shakespeare and other writers.[3] Such reading
material circulated among Montana's cattlemen, providing much-needed entertainment.

Granville Stuart, as noted in chapter 1, was willing to travel many miles to
procure books for himself, but he was also eager to share them with others.
When Stuart was a cattleman, a companion noted that Granville "thought it
would be a good thing to take a whole lot of books for the cowpunchers'
enjoyment." The audience was quite appreciative:

> The way those cowboys would tackle those books was a caution. They
> would come into camp and pick up a book and the cook would holler
> "Grub Pile" till he was red in the face and he could never get all those
> fellows to come at the same time. Just as soon as a fellow would drop a
> book some other galoot would grab it. The cook called me aside one day
> and told me he was going to quit as the boys thought more of Granville's
> books than they did of his grub. It would never do to lose a good cook at

that time in the game and I told him not to say anything and I would see that they would cause him no more trouble. It was the next day that we arrived at the Yellowstone so I gathered up the books and threw them into the river, thus starting the first circulating library ever known in Montana.[4]

Moving from Stuart's idea of a circulating library to the destruction of books circulating in the Yellowstone River is clever, but this anecdote also attests to cowboy hunger for reading that no doubt included Shakespeare.

When he wrote of the life of a cowboy in the 1920s, Philip Ashton Rollins asserted that it was not unusual to see ranch hands sitting around absolutely silent, listening to someone reading Shakespeare aloud to them. Speaking about one particular ranch near Livingston, Rollins notes that the women who visited preferred novels, but "cowboys alone attacked Shakespeare," engaging in "dramatic episodes" from the plays, turning them sometimes into "slangy paraphrase" and appreciating the intellectual vitality of Shakespeare as transmitted in a great variety of his plays. Rollins memorably described a top rider who came "face to face with the play Julius Caesar and its 'Dogs of war'" and exclaimed "'Gosh! That fellow Shakespeare could sure spill the real stuff. He's the only poet I ever seen what was fed on raw meat.'"[5] This oft-quoted anecdote is popular because it evokes the purportedly unlikely combination between poetry and the rough cattle men. Yet the more such a story is touted as unlikely, the more it becomes clear that this sort of paradox is exactly what fed fantasies of the learned cowboy in westerns yet to come.

The potential rowdiness of cowboys informs a newspaper account of their attendance at a performance of *Othello* in Livingston in 1886. Ominously, "about forty cowboys just in from the round-up marched in in single file and took seats in front of the house." They sat there quietly until Othello kissed Desdemona, at which point "the broncho riders set up a groan that sounded much like a horse afflicted with the distemper." George Miln, the actor playing Othello, grew nervous, and the newspaper writer imagines his paleness as evident under his black makeup, until he escaped to his dressing room. The Livingston newspaper read the incident as another example of "the old time terror that tenderfeet feel for the cow-punchers of the west," and from this angle it looks as though a group of prankster cowboys found it hilarious to mock a big-city actor such as George Miln.[6] At the same time, perhaps the disapproval was genuine—a way of registering discomfort with an interracial kiss (even one delivered by a white actor in blackface). Regardless, this account demonstrates that Montana cowboys were not just readers of Shakespeare but also audience members at performances of the plays in the nineteenth century. From *The Virginian* to Rollins to these rowdy spectators, the cowboys asserted their right not only to know Shakespeare but to make him into their own image.

One of Montana's "favorite sons" is cowboy artist, storyteller, and author Charlie Russell. His images of Montana landscapes in the late nineteenth and early twentieth century are characterized by sweeping scenes of horses, Natives, and cowboys in these settings. His wife, Nancy, who marketed Russell's works to make him internationally known, was also part of a Shakespeare women's club in Great Falls, Montana—one of many such clubs across the state that engaged in rigorous reading and discussions of the plays (see chapter 3). Nancy's group decided to put on a performance of *A Midsummer Night's Dream* in 1902, endeavoring to connect their environment to Shakespeare's sense of the magical forest. This outdoor production engaged intimately with the physical landscape: participants rode upon a hay wagon to a large field, where these "housewives in lacy muslin" had prepared to play all of the parts (except for Bottom, who was—beyond all expectations—played by an actual donkey). The wagon became mired in a slough and the performance was eventually rained out, but not before one of the actors confidently gestured toward the field and declared in the words of the play, "Here's a marvelous convenient place for our rehearsal!"[7] The event was memorialized in a painting by Charlie Russell with the caption: "*A Midsummer Night's Dream* turns *Tempest*, but *All's Well That Ends Well.*"[8] Russell, known for his iconic paintings of the western landscape, placed Shakespeare in this space as well—the fairies of Britain reimagined in a field outside of Great Falls. Trees and fields of Shakespeare's plays became part of the insistent expression of Montana's landscape, with the "cowboy artist" of the West sketching the event as it unfolded, subject to the elements.

Although ranching culture and lifestyles have changed a great deal over the past century, the association between cowboys and literature remains strong, nowhere more so than in cowboy poetry. These poets and musicians draw on a wide variety of literary influences, but Shakespeare is, not surprisingly, a frequent muse. Contemporary poet Rod Miller, like Wallace McRae (see prologue), appreciates the influence of Shakespeare on his artistry. Miller quotes

Figure 7. Charlie Russell's sketch of a Great Falls women's club performance of *A Midsummer Night's Dream* on May 19, 1902, that was rained out. The caption reads, "'A Midsummer Night's Dream' Turns 'Tempest,' But 'All's Well That Ends Well.'" Russell included his wife's name (Nancy B. Russell) and the date at the bottom. Photograph of sketch reproduced from *Montana: The Magazine of Western History* 22, no. 2 (1972): 54.

Rollins's anecdote about the cowboy who loved Mark Antony's "Cry havoc" speech from *Julius Caesar* (3.1.254–75), then reflects on the inspiration that such words can still give cowboy poets today:

> Let's tear down the fences, or at least open the gates. Let a mixed herd of poems and poets populate your pastures—all kinds and colors, the ordinary and the exotic, the old and the new, the easy-to-digest and those requiring rumination. It's enjoyable. It's educational. And it's well worth your time to search for a writer who can, for you, "sure spill the real stuff."[9]

Cowboy poets today, like those who first roamed through the fertile grasslands of Montana, consider Shakespeare a model for raw and meaningful writing. The quotidian experience of working on the land finds its perfect expression in the visceral encounters with Shakespearean language.

THE GOLDEN AGE

What is here? Gold? Yellow, glittering, precious gold?
—*Timon of Athens*

The explorers who came through the Northern Rockies in the first half of the nineteenth century led transient lives, constantly on the move across the broad landscape in search of animal pelts and trade routes. But eventually the central commodity changed to precious metals, and with that development arose the first permanent settlements. The gold strikes at Grasshopper Creek and Alder Gulch in 1862–1863 inaugurated the gold rush in what was incorporated as Montana Territory by President Lincoln in 1864. As is typical of gold rush communities, the settlements of Bannack, Virginia City, and other early mining towns developed rapidly and with a great deal of excitement. The Montana mining towns were especially remote, for the nearest large city, Salt Lake City, was four hundred miles away, while Denver was nearly eight hundred miles away, and of course such distances would have taken weeks to cross. The residents of these Montana towns thus had to forge their own unique communities, to build their own institutions—governmental, educational, and civic—at an accelerated pace.

These years on the frontier were volatile, to say the least, as recorded by Thomas Dimsdale, an English immigrant, schoolteacher, and newspaper editor who wrote *The Vigilantes of Montana* in 1865–1866. This work tells of the triumph of vigilantes in Virginia City's earliest years, when the corrupt road agents were brought to justice. Each chapter in Dimsdale's work opens with an epigraph that underlines its main themes, and more than a third of these epigraphs are quotations from Shakespeare's plays. For Dimsdale, Shakespeare was the perfect font of wisdom that could reinforce the cycle of villainy and just execution that is chronicled in *Vigilantes*. Shakespeare's villains, such as Macbeth, Richard III, Claudius, and Don John, thus become patterns for the road agents, who are engaged in "matter deep and dangerous," especially "Murder most foul."[1] Dimsdale asserts the rightness of the vigilantes' actions against such reprehensible figures with a quotation from *Measure for Measure*: "Thieves for their robbery have authority / When judges steal themselves."[2] Dimsdale trained his sight upon the guilt of the road agents by equating them with well-known Shakespearean murderers, quoting Macbeth's "Will all Neptune's ocean wash this blood clean from my hands?" and Claudius's "primal eldest curse" of fraternal murder.[3] But Dimsdale was less interested in the psychological torment that Shakespeare depicted than he was in broad portraits of villains who inevitably would be punished as a result of divine displeasure.

Vigilantes appeared serially in Montana Territory's first newspaper, the *Montana Post*, where subscribers could read regular installments of this arresting story.[4] Such serial publication was common in nineteenth-century America not just for current events but for literary works as well, including the classics. That the residents of Virginia City were reading serial editions of Shakespeare is confirmed by an extant copy of this type currently housed in the city's historical society archives: an 1802 volume of five Shakespearean plays (volume one of eight), accompanied by Samuel Johnson's notes, but published in Boston (see figure 9). This particular edition was designed to arrive in monthly installments, thus was packaged as the same sort of exciting publication that characterized other serials of this period.[5] This kind of Shakespeare volume in Virginia City attests to the ease with which frontier inhabitants approached his works: these were books to be purchased, read, and explored. Shakespeare might be a "classic" author, but his words were going to be mined as surely as the earth that these Virginia City residents turned over daily.

The *Montana Post* was the source of information, advertisements, and opinions in the bustling Virginia City of the 1860s. During this period there were regular ads for various establishments, including the "Shakspeare Restaurant" on Wallace Street. Regular ads in the newspaper announced this as a "first class

Figure 8. Thomas Dimsdale's one-room schoolhouse, where he taught students (including Mary Sheehan Ronan) and wrote *The Vigilantes of Montana.* The school was constructed in 1863 in Virginia City but was moved to nearby Nevada City for historic preservation by the Bovey family in 1976. Photo by Kevin Brustuen, 2019.

restaurant for the accomodation of the traveling public, as well as the public generally."[6] The first editor of the *Montana Post*, Henry N. Blake, wrote in his memoirs that the restaurant was called this because it was managed by "an Englishman bearing the name of William Shakespeare." When it became a dwelling house in 1866 Blake and his family moved in and later bought the building, at which point he "found in the attic a sign left by the first tenant on which was painted 'William Shakespeare.'" Meeting him in person a decade later, Blake surmised that this "Shakespeare" man "appeared to be a person without education [or] native ability" but was satisfied that he was in fact entitled to his surname because of descent from the famous writer—a rather misguided assumption, considering the well-established fact that Shakespeare had no direct descendants.[7] The name was probably chosen by the English restauranteur because it gave him a sort of cultural capital, or at least distinctive identity, in Virginia City. Meanwhile, as miners had to name their lodes, it was perhaps inevitable that along with a cast that included the Rough and Ready

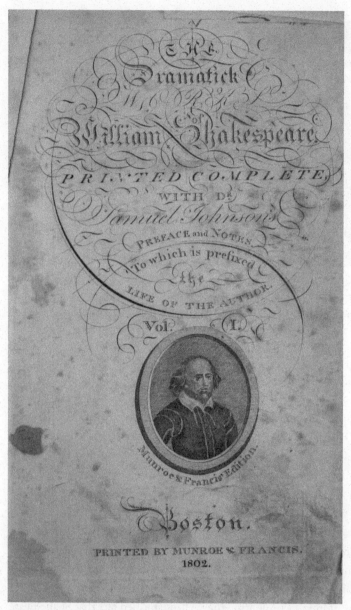

Figure 9. An 1802 edition of Shakespeare's plays from Virginia City. This
is the first volume of an eight-volume series that included notes by
Samuel Johnson and was a popular version of the plays for Americans
in the nineteenth century. The volume is part of the Dick Pace Archive
Collection at the Thompson-Hickman Madison County Library in
Virginia City. Photo by Kevin Brustuen, 2019.

Lode, the Quaker Lode, and the Red White and Blue Lode, there was in fact a Shakespeare Lode.[8]

Dimsdale's regular contributions to the *Montana Post* advocated for proper pastimes that would countermand the sinful behavior of so many mining town residents, who loved to spend time drinking, gambling, and enjoying the diversions of the "hurdy-gurdy houses."[9] Despite the rough nature of Virginia City, however, there were plenty of avenues for more "upright" activities, such as reading rooms and literary societies. The Gem Saloon in fact "housed a reading room where subscribing members enjoyed all forms of reading matter as well as chess, checkers, and dominoes."[10] In the spirit of literary and moral culture, James Duncan Sr. formed an amateur theatrical company that put on a number of plays at Junction, near Virginia City. Taking a page from Shakespeare's own time, Duncan's all-male cast solved the problem of female characters simply by "dress[ing] a boy up in our mother's dresses." The company performed *Macbeth* and other plays, and along the way they always maintained a sense of humor. Embracing the confusion of having three actors named Jack on the stage simultaneously, one of them "got his arms around the Jacks and exclaimed [echoing the witches in *Macbeth*], 'When shall we three meet again?'"[11] All the plays were free of charge and were followed by a dance that encouraged family gathering and participation. Such events attracted a wide variety of attendees, including Hezekiah Hosmer, the first chief justice of Montana Territory, whose wife and daughter performed some of their own Shakespearean skits at local social functions. A program from a Bannack in 1864 shows that two of Hosmer's children, along with four members of Governor Edgerton's family, enacted *The Tragedy of King Edward IV*—a rarely performed play by Thomas Heywood, one of Shakespeare's contemporaries.[12]

Like other mining towns before it, Virginia City quickly built those structures that promoted moral and cultural stability. They thus erected the first church in Montana Territory in November of 1864 and the first theatre the following month. DeWitt Waugh opened the Montana Theatre because it was "an absolutely necessity," as he put it, to establish "a place of innocent amusement where we can take our families without fear of insult."[13] Dimsdale approved, saying that "the theatre affords substantial gratification and innocent recreation, at much less cost" than the hurdy-gurdy houses. The Montana Theatre operated for two years and was succeeded by the People's Theatre, a two-hundred-seat venue over a billiard saloon. Despite frequent improvements, conditions at the People's Theatre were harsh; it was "a rough unpainted building" that "contained a small stage and rows of unplaned log benches," and "chilling winds blew through the uninsulated walls."[14] Nonetheless, these theatres featured a wide variety of shows, especially minstrels, musicals, and comedies, from 1864 to 1866. Sometimes actors performed scenes from Shakespeare during these years; on one occasion a local actor named Charles Graham played the role of Othello opposite Salt Lake–based actor J. S. Townsend.[15] This rendering of Act 3 from *Othello* was appreciated by some audience members in Virginia City, but E. B. Nealy told the story quite differently:

> The part [of Othello] was not well committed, and sentences were commenced with Shakespearian loftiness and ended with the actor's own emendations, which were certainly questionable improvements. Anything but a tragic effect was produced by seeing the swarthy Moor turn to the prompter at frequent intervals, and inquire, "What?" in a hoarse whisper. A running colloquy took place between Othello and his audience, in which he made good his assertion that he was rude in speech. Since then, Shakespeare has not been attempted on the Virginia boards. "Othello's occupation's gone"; and all tragic efforts are confined to the legitimate Rocky Mountain drama.[16]

The "swarthy Moor" was of course a white actor, Graham, in blackface, which was standard in nineteenth-century America. The *Montana Post* did print a short piece later in 1866, though, noting that an African American actor named Morgan Smith had immigrated to England and was playing the role of Othello in London (like Ira Aldridge before him).[17] Such a casting decision was not thinkable in Virginia City in the 1860s, but the young newspaper made it possible to imagine Othello's race as something beyond stage makeup.

Itinerant Actors

The opportunity for the citizens of Virginia City to see professionally acted Shakespearean plays in their entirety arrived in 1867 with a well-known company of itinerant players. John S. "Jack" Langrishe is credited with being the actor to open up the frontier to theatrical culture. He was born in Ireland in

Figure 10. John S. "Jack" Langrishe, the itinerant actor and theatre manager who brought professional Shakespeare productions to Montana in the 1860s and 1870s. The Denver Public Library, Western History Collection, X-19630.

1825 but immigrated to the United States at the age of twenty; after some time in New York, Langrishe moved to Central City, Colorado, where he began a successful career as an actor-manager. In the American West Langrishe gathered many acting stars of the day, performing to sold-out audiences with a repertoire that included everything from Shakespeare to melodrama to vaudeville. This endeavor was not unusual, for in nineteenth-century America "Shakespeare *was* popular entertainment," and the theatre "was a kaleidoscopic, democratic institution presenting a widely varying bill of fare to all classes and socioeconomic groups."[18]

As Colorado's gold rush began to falter, resulting in a slowing of the economy, Langrishe and his troupe sought newer gold rush towns further north. They took the long and perilous journey to Salt Lake City, hauling costumes and scenery as they traveled. As the actors made their way to Virginia City, they stopped en route to relax and enjoy some hunting and fishing. One day their mules strayed, and while searching for them, they found the partial remains of a man. The itinerant company noticed the large and symmetrical skull, with the teeth intact, and "looking at that skull, all property man Jimmy Griffith thought of was 'Yorick.' They took it with them, used the skull for Hamlet and carried it eventually back to Colorado."[19] Such a story serves as the perfect metaphor for these itinerant actors, who traveled relentlessly across the frontier in order to make the works of a dead author come to life again, often with the same clever humor that characterizes the Gravediggers' appearance in Act 5 of *Hamlet*.

Langrishe's company performed several plays in Virginia City during their first visit, including *Romeo and Juliet* and *Othello*. Accounts in the *Montana Post* portray a town hungry for such a spectacle: "To-night Othello is up," announced the paper, and "the bare announcement is enough to crowd the house to repletion."[20] This was, everyone agreed, the best theatre that these miners had ever been privileged to watch. Not every performance was greeted with unmitigated praise, however. The *Montana Post* reports, while usually enthusiastic, demonstrated a nuanced understanding of theatrical performance, of Shakespeare's drama, and of celebrity culture. The review of *Othello* was measured, admitting that it was not "a superb rendering, never before equaled on the American stage," largely because the actor playing Othello, George Pauncefort, "has unfortunately no pathos in his voice."[21] Although Pauncefort was a well-established British actor with a celebrated stage history, the residents of Virginia City seemed to think that his style was too declamatory, too untrue to the emotions that the play should elicit.[22] *Othello* was one of the most popular plays in performance during this period, so the audience members had the privilege of seeing multiple renditions of this tragedy; the pathos that they expected from the Moor was unsatisfying to this Virginia City audience, perhaps in keeping with Helene Koon's assertion that the miners felt a kinship with the larger-than-life Shakespearean characters, because "their own quest for gold, their hardships, the very scenery around them was larger than the world they had known back East, and they could see their own feelings mirrored in the powerful emotions."[23] The *Montana Post* reviewers found much more to praise in another star, Mrs. Langrishe, especially in her role as Juliet, because although the actress seemed a bit old for the part, on stage she became a "sprightly, coquettish girl, with all the appearance of a boarding school miss in love for the first time, face as bright as a May morning, and every movement girlish in the extreme," and thus she assumed the part "with a perfection seldom equaled."[24] Such detailed descriptions of actors' portrayals point to the deep interest these Virginia City audiences had in seeing performances that reflected their notions of how Shakespeare *should* be staged. This was also a modern-dress production of *Romeo and Juliet*—an unusual choice at this time, and one indicative of a desire to present the play not as a distant museum piece but instead as a contemporary story that spoke to 1860s audiences.[25]

The Langrishe company's featured repertoire allowed for a mix of comedy and tragedy, and of course melodrama, which was the most popular genre of the late nineteenth century. Langrishe often gave his audience a taste for all of these genres in the course of one evening, mounting productions of plays such as *Othello* and *Macbeth*, with all their tragic grandeur, but then following them with a vaudeville short show. Langrishe was able to shine in these entertainments, for he was frequently dubbed the "comedian of the frontier" and was especially appreciated for his uncanny ability to make funny faces while acting. Such theatrical traditions have continued to the present day in Virginia City, where the Virginia City Players, the oldest continually running stock theatre company in the northwest (begun in 1948) still plays vaudeville and nineteenth-century scripts.[26] This company delights its tourist audiences with plays that echo the entertainments of the early mining days, when fun could be had by watching talented actors go back and forth between the shifting registers of the theatre.

Mining towns were marked by excitement and spontaneity, but with that came a longing for the traditions of the places from which the settlers came.[27] Shakespeare was one avenue by which they could forge cultural continuity, making the miners feel that they were indeed a vital part of a continuing story. One account of a performance by Langrishe's company in Helena in 1867 also demonstrates what it meant to be excluded from the communities created through shared appreciation of the drama. The United States marshal and his deputies wanted to attend the tragedy that was on that night (almost certainly one of Shakespeare's), so they took their prisoner with them, a Native man who had been arrested for illegal liquor sales. During the performance, "all went well until the actors started killing each other 'in great shape.' The prisoner, thinking it all in earnest, became frightened, jumped through a window onto the porch, ran to his horse, and dashed away."[28] This narration, written in the 1960s and based on nineteenth-century accounts, betrays a Euro-American trope about the Natives' failure to grasp civilized activities. It is hard to believe, in fact, that a Native person who had been around enough Euro-Americans to be arrested for illegal liquor sales would not have recognized a play. Ultimately, the joke at the expense of the unlearned Native serves as an uncomfortable metaphor for what it meant to "civilize" the frontier: the "savages" needed to exit, leaving the theatres and their accompanying cultural activities to do the work of creating a stable and lawful community.

Langrishe's troupe came regularly to Virginia City, Helena, and some other Montana mining towns once or twice a year in the late 1860s and early 1870s, providing regular entertainment, as well as one of Helena's first opera houses, named for Langrishe.[29] When the company presented *Hamlet* in Helena in 1868, the reviewer wrote:

> The gret [*sic*] play of Hamlet, possessing in itself such sterling merit that it never becomes old, was well presented last night. Mr. Waldron, with that quick conception of dramatic effects which has insured him such a favorable reception from our citizens, gave such a rendering of Hamlet as brought clearly out all the beauties of the great Shakespearean character.[30]

The portrayal of Shakespeare's epic heroes was dependent upon the exaggerated acting that was popular in the nineteenth century.[31] The actors, like their stories, needed to be expansive enough to fill up the bare stages of Montana, so the audiences were attracted to plays and performances that conveyed a sense of beauty, greatness, and purpose.

Reactions to these characters were also strongly linked to the personality cult of the itinerant actors—perhaps precisely because they appeared in town, impersonated characters, and then faded into the landscape again, leaving behind fans who wanted to know where these actors had come from and where they were going next. Most of the actors from this period were from Europe. Langrishe himself came from Ireland, and two of the prominent stars from his troupe, Charles Couldock and George Pauncefort, were English. The emigrant makeup of this theatre was an excellent match for Virginia City, a place that had been created out of thin air (or gold dust) within weeks of the Alder Gulch strike. A company comprised of artists with different origins and accents turned out to be conducive to the power of Shakespearean theatre to bring diverse peoples together. The newspapers, as the audience members, followed the careers of these itinerant performers diligently. Given the number of miles that Langrishe and his compatriots traveled, it was probably no exaggeration that, as one observer wrote, "there is scarcely an old-timer living in the West who has not heard of or seen old Jack Langrishe."[32] Actors such as Couldock and Pauncefort enjoyed longtime fame in Montana, for decades later newspapers were nostalgically printing their biographies. After leaving Langrishe's company, Pauncefort traveled throughout the West solo (perhaps in an attempt to avoid multiple lawsuits for bigamy). During these tours, he delighted audiences by reading Dickens and Shakespeare in churches, lodges, barrooms, and on the streets, from Fort Shaw to Boise to British Columbia.[33] The Helena papers continued to trace his adventures, as he eventually sailed for the Sandwich Isles, Hong Kong, and Japan. The actors who brought life to Shakespearean characters became a vital part of entertainment and culture in the mining communities, but they also remained members of those fragile societies, no matter how far away they wandered.

Langrishe's success owed as much to his personality and his understanding of what the people wanted as it did to his talents as a thespian.[34] Thus his plays were never bawdy, there was a rule against swearing in his theatres, they never performed on Sundays, and he donated some of his proceeds to organizations such as the widows and orphans fund.[35] Today, readers of Shakespeare might well wonder how performances of these plays could avoid being bawdy. The answer is that Langrishe and other performers in the nineteenth century were using bowdlerized versions of the plays that removed improper or offensive material, such as blasphemy, sexual innuendos, and allusions to suicide.[36] Langrishe himself was dedicated to the Episcopal Church and saw his life as an actor as commensurate with his religion. He was friends with bishops Daniel Tuttle and Ethelbert Talbot, and the latter reflected that Langrishe "was a lover of good books, a student and interpreter of Shakespeare, and possessed brilliant conversational gifts." Langrishe appreciated the beauty of the Bible and the Book of Common Prayer, and he also recognized the value of performance in the pulpit. As an act of friendship, he used his expertise by giving several prominent clergymen lessons in elocution. Talbot remembered that Langrishe could render a worship service "with an impressiveness and appreciation rarely found."[37] Such accounts of Langrishe make it clear that he saw theatre as part of a mission to bring a moralizing and civilizing force to the lawless and notoriously sinful mining towns—a goal that Dimsdale appreciated.

Langrishe's troupe was substantially composed of families, for he always traveled with his wife, just as Couldock always traveled and performed with his daughter Eliza. Family connections helped the troupes to convey the idea that theatre is not in fact transient but a symbol of urban permanence. A young woman such as Eliza elicited a great deal of appreciation from the largely male audience. The townspeople regularly organized benefit performances (supplemental performances in which the featured actor keeps the proceeds to compensate for insufficient salary). At one point Eliza was the recipient of one such benefit, where she was presented a twenty-ounce gold nugget worth $450. The *Montana Post* hailed this occasion as a tribute to Eliza's ability to touch "a tender chord in the heart of the digger and delver in the ground."[38] In a similar tribute, Montanans presented Langrishe with a "brick" of gold worth over $500 just before he departed for a return trip to Colorado—an impressive reminder that these northern audiences were grateful and would patiently await his next visit.[39]

Looking at the map of places visited by Langrishe and the itinerant actors that traveled with him, one is struck by the geographical scope of their profession—not just that they reached many different towns but that they crisscrossed the West so many times. The Langrishes went back and forth between destinations as far apart as Denver, Helena, New Orleans, Chicago, Salt Lake, Deadwood, and Coeur d'Alene. The constant movement of the actors mirrored the quickly shifting nature of frontier towns that were dependent upon the mining economies. During gold booms the excitement and spontaneity lent themselves to celebratory atmospheres, and theatre became part of that. Each time the players returned to Montana, residents of Virginia City, Diamond City, Helena, and Deer Lodge were enthusiastic; during Langrishe's return to Helena in 1883, "throngs of Montanans . . . waited in hotels, eager for the first handshake."[40] By this time travel was also easier, for the actors were able to travel via the Northern Pacific Railroad; indeed, the frontier was now connected through the emerging economy enabled by the "iron horse."

Given the profound impact that Langrishe had on several mining communities, it is surprising to witness his own forlorn words about the profession of acting: "Your words do not live like the poets or the painters, to be seen or read by everyone. ... The actor's art is different, 'He struts his brief hour upon the stage and then is heard no more.'"[41] Remarkably, the words are Macbeth's, and the endurance of Shakespeare resonates, even as Langrishe himself worries that he will fade from memory.[42] When he did pass away in 1895 in Idaho, the newspapers of the Rockies were filled with reports of Langrishe's death. A Leadville, Colorado, newspaper aptly quoted from *1 Henry IV*: "Could not all this flesh keep in a little life? Poor Jack, farewell! We could have better spared a better man."[43] By the time he died there were many other itinerant actors who regularly came through the West, but Langrishe was remembered as the first, and often as the most beloved.

Diverse Audiences

Other than the reports from the newspaper reviews, we have few extant comments from those who attended the plays in mining camps. In the reminiscences of A. K. McClure, a traveler through Montana Territory in 1867, however, each evening was full of life. He noted that the theatre was directed by "the jolly Langrishe," and between acts everyone went to the "Pony" saloon opposite to "clear the cobwebs" out of their throats between acts. McClure wrote that "pleasure and business are happily mingled in Western life," which is what he experienced when he "had a truce of a week with the mountains and mines."[44] Granville Stuart, that avid reader of Shakespeare (see chapter 1), apparently did not attend a Shakespeare performance until he took a trip to St. Louis in 1866 and saw *King Lear* and *Hamlet*, both of which disappointed because of the "blood and thunder acting" of Edwin Forrest.[45] Stuart must have been in the audience when the Langrishe company performed Shakespeare in Virginia City the following year, joining the usual activities, for as McClure attested, "Pretty much everybody [went] to the theatre."[46]

During the 1860s, Stuart was friends with a family named the Daltons, and he began calling their eldest daughter Desdemona because "she was beautiful and so good."[47] Meanwhile, Stuart's next-door neighbors, the Sheehans, had a little girl named Mary who was raised in a series of mining camps. She had what might be considered a lawless upbringing, for she spent time sneaking out of Dimsdale's school, saw some of the hangings of the road agents and other criminals, and dredged out the long, narrow sluice boxes of the mines, attempting to recover some gold from the placer gravel. Nonetheless, Mary noted that "even during our residence in Alder Gulch, so wild, so isolated from civilization, we had Shakespeare's plays, some of Scott's romances, and Moore's and Byron's poems."[48] Their cabin in Helena (to which they moved after their stint in Virginia City) had domestic touches such as muslin curtains, calico coverings for the chairs, and braided rag rugs, yet, "commanding the scene, more dominating even than the heating stove, was the 'stand' covered with a bright-colored throw. Our kerosene lamp was in the center and grouped around it were books. We always had a prayer book and a little testament, selected plays of Shakespeare, and collected poems."[49] In Helena in 1867, Mary was doing dramatic readings in school, so she diligently practiced her part, Lady Anne from *Richard III*, in front of the mirror, "trying a variety of interpretations from mincing to flamboyant." Mary's stepmother put a stop to this vain activity, because she "became now positively alarmed for the salvation of my soul and forbade me to go on with the practices." Nonetheless, Mary longed to attend the theatre whenever she could, remarking in a conscious echo of *Hamlet* that "for me the play was the thing."[50]

Mary Sheehan Ronan's story shows the power of theatre to encourage spectators to identify with characters, and everything we know about the responses of audiences in mining towns suggests that they all had a tendency to do the same. Reflecting upon the parallels that these readers and viewers of Shakespeare in the American West may have noticed, Andrew Dickson wonders whether "Shakespeare's titanic dramas of kings and queens, heroes and villains, found some kind of resonance with hard-bitten frontier communities, accustomed to a life of extremes."[51] What is missing from the historical record, however, is any self-conscious reflection on this identification that would enhance our understanding of *how* Shakespeare was read and understood during this period. We do not know, for instance, what Granville Stuart might have thought about *Othello*, considering that he was married to a Native American woman. After all, racial diversity was not unusual in Virginia City, which had several prominent black citizens, so the plight of Othello need not have been understood in the abstract.[52] At the other extreme, numerous accounts report that it took ten days for news of Lincoln's assassination to reach Virginia City, and when they finally heard many of the citizens (including Mary Ronan) danced in the streets with joy.[53] That same year, Langrishe's company performed *Macbeth*, and it is difficult to imagine that no one thought

Figure 11. Mary Sheehan Ronan around the time of her marriage in 1873. She was raised in Virginia City and Helena in a household that owned a prized volume of Shakespeare. Photo number 83.0138. Archives and Special Collections, Mansfield Library, University of Montana.

about the assassinated president when the Macbeths slaughtered Duncan.[54] A history of Shakespeare from this period, though, is related in anecdotes, reviews, and reminiscences. Not surprisingly, none of these genres are conducive to contemporary reflections upon race or politics. Instead, we must be attuned to very different sorts of messages, read between a nineteenth-century penchant for humor and burlesque.

One account of an Independence Day celebration in Helena in 1866 does provide insight of this sort. As the *Montana Post* reported, "In the evening, the theatres seemed to recognize the fitness of winding up a day that had been filled with burlesque from dawn to eve, with some more of the same sort. Accordingly, at the Helena Theatre, 'Richard III' was presented, riding on a live jackass."[55] Such a raucous celebration and mockery of Richard's horse hardly had any serious purpose, but even so, the relationship between

celebrating American independence and mocking British oppression by tyr-
anny remains under the surface of this farce.

Other interactions between actors and audience members show a complex
negotiation of sexual politics on the frontier, as evidenced by the remarkable
story of Laura Honey Agnes Stevenson, the daughter of a well-known London actress. Stevenson herself reputedly sang the Shakespearean song "Over
Hill over Dale"[56] in London under Charles Kean when she was young, but
later the talented singer and actress became nearly destitute, traveling throughout the American West in the 1860s and 1870s accompanied only by her
husband-manager—a mysterious man named Professor Church who was described as a "little pinched-up fellow . . . with a face that would drive away
rather than draw an audience."[57] Stevenson was remembered in particular for
her one-woman performance of the balcony scene in *Romeo and Juliet*. In the
absence of an actor to be Romeo, she employed "a dummy clothing figure
such as is frequently seen in front of the 'gents' furnishing stores . . . sur-
mounted by a handsome blockhead," with a rich velvet cap, cloak, and feath-
ers.[58] This performance was a burlesque of the balcony scene, interspersed
with piano playing and singing for further entertainment; the newspaper ad-
vertised it as "Opera Mad! Opera Mad! Or, Romeo and Juliet."[59] The miners
called Stevenson "Julio" and loved it when "she made love to Romeo after a
style that kept the house in a continuous roar."[60]

Shortly after the Deer Lodge performance, Stevenson remounted the same
show in the neighboring placer camp of Pioneer, with equal success: "The
scene was given with great eclat, the applause was tumultuous. It was Shakespeare's introduction to a Pioneer audience. It was enjoyed . . . [and] was
unanimously agreed upon that the Honey Stevenson show was a hummer."[61]
Leaving the performance hall and migrating to the saloon, the rowdy miners
of Pioneer took the Romeo dummy with them and "forced" him to carouse
with them all night; the damage was substantial, for "his red shirt was torn to
shreds, his nose bit off, his eyes gouged out and his cheeks smashed in."[62]
Sheepishly, the miners returned the remains of "Rummy" to Stevenson, who
wailed in a dramatic performance of grief:

Dead, dead, dead, my Romeo, my Romeo, speak to me this once; tell me
you love me; it can not be that he is dead; Romeo, Romeo, my darling
Romeo; yes, yes, he is dead, dead. O Romeo, Romeo, speak—[63]

This performance, which sounds in tone and action so much like Thisbe's lament over the dead body of Pyramus in *A Midsummer Night's Dream* (5.1.317–40), was first so sorrowful, and then so appreciated for its histrionics, that the miners raised more than enough funds for her to replace her most prized prop. Stevenson continued to entertain on stages in Helena, Missoula, and beyond, but the story of that infamous performance as Juliet remained strong in Montana theatre lore. The story circulated widely, appearing in newspapers in New York, Kansas, and Oregon, adding a mythological quality to what it meant for people on the Montana frontier to encounter Shakespeare.

When theatrical impresario John Maguire reflected upon this famous legend in the *Anaconda Standard* in 1898, he told it against the background of the excitement of those gold-rush communities, where "the Thespian had to move his cart to fresh fields and pastures new," but the effort was worth it. They prospered because "it was refreshing to the people to have something beyond and above their own little improvised entertainments to break the monotony of the long nights." Using Shakespeare's celebrated description of Brutus, Maguire called Jack Langrishe "the noblest Roman of them all" (*Julius Caesar*, 5.5.69), who strode onto the stages, as did the other itinerant actors, in primitive conditions. Maguire went on to write:

> I often think that the performances of those days, given, as they were, with the most crude surroundings, were to the people of that time much more pleasurable and delightful than are the most artistic performances of many celebrities to our blasé audiences of the present.[64]

The recounting of the Laura Honey Stevenson story hearkens back to a golden age where all things seemed possible—even quality, and hilarious, Shakespearean entertainment courtesy of a single actress and a mannequin.

Ghost Towns

Gold rushes create settlements overnight, but once the supply of precious metal runs out, these towns collapse almost as quickly as they were erected. As a result, Montana, like many places in the West, is dotted with ghost towns. Pioneer is one such, as is Bannack. Another ghost town is Kendall (located near Lewistown), which was established in 1901 around a cyanide gold recovery plant and gold mining operation. Kendall flourished for only a decade, then quickly declined; by 1921 it was uninhabited. In its heyday there were two newspapers; one of these, the *Kendall Miner*, published regular columns about Shakespeare—historical tidbits, news from international papers, and reflections upon the wisdom of his words. There were also jokes, such as the riddle "What character in Shakespeare's works killed the greatest number of chickens?" The answer: "Hamlet's uncle, because he did 'murder most foul.'"[65] The comfortable familiarity of these columns corroborates what a historian of nearby Lewistown wrote of this period:

> The amazing thing to an outsider was the culture to be found in a little town far out in the heart of the boundless prairies. There seemed to be more than a fair sprinkling of highly educated men and women who for some good and honorable reason had unfettered their souls in the wilderness.[66]

Even though these residents reveled in their sense of open spaces, however, they were quick to invest in the civic and municipal. In 1906 Kendall's Shakespearean interests were reflected by its large bank, which ran a regular ad:

> There is a bank whereon the wild thyme grows. —Shakespeare
> Here is the bank wherein your odd change grows.[67]

Such an interweaving of a (slightly altered) quotation from *A Midsummer Night's Dream* and the promise of profit demonstrates that the residents of Kendall were the kind of people who would appreciate the clever advertising scheme. Mining town banks were of course prominent businesses, functioning as a symbol as well as a practical place where one could store and grow the fortune that the gold-seekers hoped to accumulate. Later that year, the paper poked gentle fun at the head cashier of this bank, Mr. Henderson, who had recently married (perhaps a shotgun wedding) and was said to have a copy of *Taming of the Shrew* on his desk for reference. He was even, the report joked, running classes at the bank because of his expertise in the notorious play about controlling one's unruly wife. Such regular Shakespearean references thus accompany an array of the lived experiences in this mining town, from

Figure 12. The remains of the Kendall bank that ran a Shakespeare-inspired advertising campaign in the first decade of the twentieth century. Kendall is now a ghost town. Photo by Kevin Brustuen, 2017.

capital acquisition to marriage. Meanwhile, the gazebo that stood in the center of the town likewise attested to the Kendall residents' appetite for entertainment at the foot of the mountains that held wealth, just below the surface.

Some walls of this crumpled bank are still visible today in the ghost town of Kendall, which sits at the base of hills scarred by mining. People lived here for a short time, but in Kendall, as in the rest of Montana, the residents had Shakespeare by their sides. In the restless movements of these settlers during the "golden age" of mining, Shakespeare symbolized permanence, for his cultural legacy was more stable than the boom and bust economies of mineral extraction.

INTERLUDE 2
CIPHERS

And let us, ciphers to this great account,
On your imaginary forces work.

—*Henry V*

When Montana became a territory in 1864, Abraham Lincoln appointed Hezekiah Hosmer as its first chief justice. He and his family traveled the arduous journey from their home in Ohio, making their way to Montana via the Missouri River with an army escort. They lived in the territorial capital, Virginia City, for the four years during which he served as chief justice and then another three during which he served as the capital's postmaster. Hosmer was involved in the social and civic life of Montana; he was a member of the Masons, frequently attended theatrical performances with his family in both Helena and Virginia City, and his wife and daughter gave Shakespearean recitations at various literary events, not just in their home town, but in Butte, Helena, and Dillon.[1] Hosmer was certainly a man of letters, and he loved Shakespeare—or rather, he loved the works attributed to the middle-class man from Stratford-upon-Avon. After he retired to San Francisco, Hosmer wrote a book that explained his belief about these works; in *Bacon and Shakespeare in the Sonnets* (1887) he put forth a theory that Shakespeare's plays were in fact written by Sir Francis Bacon and the sonnets contained a cipher that could be seen to express this authorial truth.[2] This book was the culmination of many years of study, for as Montana entertainer and writer Larry Barsness wryly notes, in 1860s Virginia City, "literary societies flourished and withered each winter after listening to one of Judge Hosmer's presentations of the reasons Bacon was Shakespeare."[3]

Such theories were not original to Hosmer, for the nineteenth century gave rise to a movement doubting the authorship of Shakespeare's works—a position referred to as anti-Stratfordian because of its assertion that the man from Stratford-upon-Avon did not write the works attributed to him. The case for Bacon's authorship had first been championed by East Coast writer and scholar Delia Bacon in the 1850s, and her work gained acclaim from a surprising array of literary figures, including Walt Whitman, Harriet Beecher Stowe, Ralph Waldo Emerson, and especially Mark Twain. Twain himself was a friend of Hosmer's, and the two corresponded on several occasions.[4] Around the time that Hosmer was completing his work on Bacon and Shakespeare, Twain was publishing a landmark work by Minnesota congressman Ignatius Donnelly entitled *The Great Cryptogram* (1888).[5] This one-thousand-page book proposed that there is a mathematically complex cryptogram embedded within the works of Shakespeare; interpreted correctly, this cryptogram points to the hidden biography of Bacon. In this reading, Bacon was like Prospero, the protagonist of *The Tempest*, a magnanimous ruler who was unjustly cast down but whose powers remained immense. Donnelly's cryptogram was notoriously difficult to understand, but his work was popular enough to gain national attention for the Bacon theory, so he traveled widely to speak about his beliefs.

In 1893, Donnelly came to Butte to lecture on *The Great Cryptogram* to a sold-out crowd at Maguire's Opera House. He scoffed at the notion that William Shakespeare could have written these lofty poetic works—a man who couldn't even spell his own name and was "in his youth . . . a ruffian and a drunkard, and had to escape to London to avoid being hung for killing a deer."[6] While Donnelly was touring to give lectures on Bacon, a physician from Detroit, Orville Ward Owen, was completing his own six-volume anti-Stratfordian work, called *Sir Francis Bacon's Cipher Story*. Unlike Donnelly's obscure cipher that seemed to have no system that could be understood, Owen's cipher was supported by a tangible decoding machine "consisting of two large drums on which revolved a two-foot-wide and thousand-foot-long canvass sheet."[7] Works that Owen attributed to Bacon (including those of Shakespeare, Edmund Spenser, Robert Burton, and others) were pasted on the wheel, and as the drum spun, key words revealed secret messages. The biography of Bacon that emerged from Owen's wheel (also called the Shakespeare Mangle) was much more complex and scandalous than the previous anti-Stratfordians asserted: Bacon was the illegitimate son of Queen Elizabeth and the Earl of Leicester and thus the rightful heir to the throne, but before the Queen could acknowledge him, she was strangled to death by the powerful statesman Robert Cecil.[8] As if this tabloid-style story weren't enough, the *Missoula Weekly Gazette* reported that "the most thrilling narrative is that relating to the murder and decapitation of poor Shakespeare," who attempted to extort money from Bacon for publishing works under his name: "The player was insolent in his demands, and in the heat of passion Bacon drew his sword and killed him. Before the blood was washed from his hands a gentleman appeared and asked what he had done. 'Killed a dog,' was Bacon's reply."[9] As this and other Montana newspapers reported, Owen was on an expedition to Britain that had been directed by his cipher machine: he was looking for the lost manuscripts of Bacon and the lost head of Shakespeare. Both of these, the cipher had informed Owen, could be located by dredging up the banks of the River Wye near the Welsh border.

Such conspiracies and ciphers may sound strange from a modern perspective, but gentlemen scientists such as Donnelly and Owen were part of nineteenth-century intellectual culture, and many respected their ideas about improbabilities like Atlantis.[10] But what did the Montana audience think of the Bacon theories? Montana newspapers frequently reported on Donnelly's lectures and on Owen's expeditions, but these accounts never included an endorsement of the cipher mania. In a review of Hosmer's *Bacon and Shakespeare in the Sonnets*, a Helena reporter encourages readers to buy the book, which is "beautifully written," but includes the caveat, "If we could only believe that Shakespeare was not a heaven-born genius and the author of the plays that go by his name, the explanations in [Hosmer's] volume would have great force." But ultimately, argues the reviewer, the particulars of the case run contrary to historical evidence and plausibility.[11] Actor Frederick Warde was much less measured in his criticism, scoffing that he "would as soon repudiate the authorship of the Lord's Prayer as to ascribe the writings of Shakespeare to any other man."[12] What is at stake for those who take positions on this

Figure 13. Orville Ward Owen's "Cipher Wheel." The machine, which included one thousand feet of canvas covered with works written in sixteenth- and seventeenth-century England, was used by Owen to demonstrate that Sir Francis Bacon wrote the plays and poems attributed to Shakespeare. Photo reproduced from Orville W. Owen, *Sir Francis Bacon's Cipher Story*, vol. 2 (1894).

controversy is the question of where great fiction comes from. As James Shapiro notes, Twain's conviction that Shakespeare couldn't have written the plays was driven by his belief that fiction always derives from personal experiences, so the autobiography must match the writing. For someone like Warde, however, what mattered was the transcendent moral and aesthetic quality of Shakespeare's plays. "Read Bacon and not a line of poetry will you discover," said Warde, but "read Shakespeare and the poetry therein is as beautiful as the dew drops that glisten on the green grass in the sunlit morning."[13] The messy, transcendent poetry, argued Warde, was sublime and entirely different from Bacon's rational and scientific writings.

A voice similar to Warde's emerged in another Butte lecture from the 1890s, this time addressed to the fraternal order Woodmen of the World. The lecturer, A. B. Keith, began by saying, "I have little faith in the 'Cryptogram' of Ignatius Donnelly, written to rear a slumbering doubt as to poetic ideals of the past,"[14] for "the works of Shakespeare must rest upon their merits, regardless of their authorship, and invite applause or censure as they influence the conduct of men." The speech Keith gave was a detailed exposition of *Hamlet* arguing that the play was not an author's biography but a profound treatise on human nature, for "the Hamlet of Shakespeare, the Hamlet of human nature—lives forever in the literature of the world."[15]

The Bacon authorship theory has largely fallen by the wayside, replaced by other anti-Stratfordian conspiracies, most notably those pointing to Edward de Vere, Earl of Oxford.[16] Meanwhile, cryptogram puzzles have likewise fallen into obscurity, and we might assume that Owen's cipher wheel ended up buried, too, like the lost Bacon manuscripts and the head for which Owen vainly dug on the banks of the Wye. Yet at the turn of the twenty-first century, this Shakespeare mangle was unexpectedly resurrected. An independent scholar named Virginia Fellows followed the trail of Baconian authorship theories and found Owen's cipher wheel in a warehouse in Detroit.[17] Fellows bought the mangle on the condition that she would give it to some organization for safekeeping, and before her death she did indeed bequeath it to Summit University—the educational center run by the Church Universal and Triumphant (CUT) in Gardiner, Montana.

Why would this New Age religious organization want a Baconian cipher wheel? On one level, the conspiracy theories and belief in hidden codes on which the anti-Stratfordians thrive share something in common with this kind of organization, which tends toward apocalyptic paranoia that leads them to stockpile weapons and build fallout shelters. The editors' preface to Fellows's book taps into this notion of "a great persecution" that has covered the truth; Bacon's story, they argue, is one of "destiny denied, secrets that could not be told."[18] The CUT's interest in Francis Bacon is more specific, however, for they include him as part of their pantheon. According to their teachings, the spirit of Saint Germain, the theosophical inspiration behind much of CUT's doctrines, has been reincarnated throughout history, in personages such as the Virgin Mary, Buddha, Merlin, Henry Wadsworth Longfellow, and Sir Francis Bacon.[19] Bacon's inclusion on this list owes much more to his imaginative utopian work *New Atlantis* than it does to his scientific outlook, thus Fellows sees in this remarkable author's deliberate hiding of his messages to be discovered later a perfect millennial dream: "This twenty-first century promises to be a time of many disclosures."[20]

In 2019, CUT was still laying out the case for Bacon's authorship, sponsoring a talk in Bozeman called "Finding Bacon in Hamlet" that promised to reveal "the hidden life of the true author" by using film clips, live theatre, and dynamic readings from cipher.[21] While Montana as a whole has always remained suspicious of this particular theory, the state is notoriously large enough to provide a home for fringe groups because it offers the isolation to live "off the grid" and to develop nonmainstream philosophies. It is thus not surprising that, 150 years after Hosmer told Montana territory citizens that Bacon was Shakespeare, some Montanans still adhere to this conspiracy theory and work to decode the ciphers.

WOMEN'S ROLES

When all pageants of delight were played,
Our youth got me to play the woman's part.

—*Two Gentlemen of Verona*

In 1891, a group of women from Dillon, Montana, picnicked in Sheep Creek Canyon, where one read aloud a letter she had received from her sister. The letter spoke of a Shakespeare club that a group of women had formed in Kentucky. Inspired by the report of this club's success, the picnicking Dillon women discussed this idea and decided to form a club of their own. As a later club historian put it, "The letter, the suggestion, the picnic, too, perhaps, furnished inspiration, and the outcome was the Shakespeare Club."[1] This club, which is still active today, continues to bear the Shakespearean label, although most of the reading list is now more contemporary. Nevertheless, like many of its kind, this club started with the intention of studying the works of Shakespeare.

In the late nineteenth century, women accounted for a small percentage of Montana's population, even in growing urban centers.[2] Whereas the mountain men had carried Shakespeare as they crisscrossed the state in exploration, the sparse population of women appropriated him, not surprisingly, as a necessary tool in the domestification of their new home. The women's club movement began in the East in the late 1860s and gradually moved westward.

By the early 1890s, following quickly on the heels of Montana's statehood, there were clubs in at least five locations across the state, several of which took names inspired by Shakespeare, such as the West Side Shakespeare Club of Butte, the Dillon Shakespeare Club, and the As You Like It Club of Missoula. Over the next decade, dozens of women's clubs were formed, in just about every permanent settlement. Shakespeare was the inspiration for the title and the curriculum in towns from Great Falls to Billings, from Lewistown to Miles City. The Montana Federation of Women's Clubs, an affiliate of the national federation, was founded in 1904; many of the clubs joined this central organization, anxious to become part of a national community of like-minded women.

Early accounts of literary clubs in Montana emphasize the primitive conditions in which they began. Jane Croly, the earliest historian of the women's club movement in America, surveyed the activity in Montana and wrote that she was impressed that in a "state of magnificent distances" women had managed to forge clubs, despite the "sparse and scattered populations . . . separated by mountains and mines, by rivers and ravines, by rock-bound territory and limitless extent of plain."[3] Writing in 1901, W. J. Christie, herself an active club member in Butte, wrote with pride that "the Montana young woman is a splendid type of femininity. She is not only blessed with a fine physique, but is possessed of a moral and mental strength not to be surpassed by the young women of other states."[4] Like the story about the women in Dillon who were hiking in Sheep Creek Canyon, these accounts highlight just how close the study of literature was to a real and prolonged engagement with the elements.

The negotiation between frontier and drawing room may have been difficult, but the women of Montana reveled in the paradoxes. The formation of the Deer Lodge women's club, which may have been the first in the state, is a case in point. The town was also home to Montana's first college, which was founded in 1878, but a decade later the women still found Deer Lodge a decidedly new community in need of "settling." Histories of the club relate that these early women walked to and from meetings on the street, for there were no sidewalks. They carried lanterns, for there were no streetlights. And they had to buy their own cords of wood so they could keep the fire burning in the Masonic lodge where they met.[5] Yet a great deal changed, and quickly, in Montana in the ensuing decade. By 1903, the streets of the bustling city of Butte were certainly lit.[6] A visitor from New York who traveled to meet the club members in Butte recalled, "All along the sides were wooden buildings with 'store fronts,' bright lighted, and thronged with men. Most of them were saloons. Just as we came abreast of one of them an explosion rent the air. The building toppled like a house of cards."[7] The explosion was part of the labor riots—a sign of the tumultuous times and social inequalities of early twentieth-century Butte. The varied circumstances of these anecdotes, which show some women treading dark streets in a primitive town and others pushing through crowded streets in a politically charged mining city, illustrate the diverse challenges of constructing drawing-room literary societies in turn-of-the-century Montana.

Forming these clubs ultimately enabled the women to negotiate not only between public and private space but also between wilderness and civilization, to form a new identity. Shakespeare, speaking loudly in the American West since the time of the mountain men, helped these women to engage in educational pursuits, while also considering political and civic issues of their time. Like Beatrice in *Much Ado about Nothing*, these readers of Shakespeare took on a variety of roles and found their own "lady tongues."[8]

Programs

Tracing the history of the women's club movement across the United States, Katherine Scheil notes that "starting a Shakespeare reading club was a way of reestablishing a cultural life from a former place of residence and an important part of community building."[9] In Montana, the clubs were almost invariably formed by women who had moved to Montana from the East, such as Mary Hooker of Connecticut, founder of the Dillon Shakespeare Club and a relative of Harriet Beecher Stowe, or Mrs. Wickes of New York, who "founded the little society [Helena's Fortnightly Club] in the realization that social and literary activities for young girls were somewhat limited in those years."[10] There were curricular aids available nationally to guide women through the study of literature, such as the Bay View, Chautauqua, and Macaulay correspondence courses. Some clubs used these as a curricular guide, and they also brought in guest speakers, usually professors from the state colleges. At other times the women were able to take advantage of actors' expertise. The popular actor Frederick Warde, for instance, spoke at a reception sponsored by the West Side Shakespeare Club, which the newspaper described as "one of the most brilliant social functions ever witnessed in Butte."[11]

In general, however, these women were self-directed and self-taught. Their yearly programs and weekly meetings show a deep level of engagement with the literature they wanted to discuss. Each meeting began with roll call, during which the women were expected to respond with a quotation from the play they were studying.[12] Usual activities included reading aloud from the plays, engaging in discussion, and focusing on the presentation of a paper that was composed and read aloud by a group member. As a representative example, the program from the West Side Shakespeare Club of Butte in 1899–1900 gives a sense of how much ground these women covered. Over the course of that year, they read and discussed eleven Shakespeare plays: most of the history plays, plus *Merchant of Venice, Julius Caesar*, and *The Winter's Tale*. The papers written and presented by the women included character sketches, historical background (such as a report on Cicero for *Julius Caesar* and Joan of Arc for *Henry VI*). There were also papers on Henry V as a warrior and churchman and on the House of Commons in the time of Henry IV. An analogous program for Helena's Fortnightly Club in 1896–1897 prints the week's discussion questions, such as: "Did Henry V justify his father's usurpation?"; "Does Richard [III] ever have the sympathy of his readers?"; and "What is the strongest element in Iago's success in ensnaring Othello?"[13] Sometimes the women staged debates on these questions, always seeking to further their understanding of complex issues. As one member of the Dillon Shakespeare Club put it, "I have liked [the club] well because its aim has been to do things well.... I have heard statements that it is equal to a college course. Be that as it may, it is adult education and inspiration and fellowship."[14] Community-building through the shared work of intellectual pursuits is a theme that emerges repeatedly when these women reflect upon the benefit and purpose of their clubs.

The clubs were serious about the level of study required, even going so far as to impose fines on those who did not spend enough time studying, or to expel members who were not exhibiting a serious devotion to the intellectual requirements. Club membership tended to be limited, and often exclusionary; members were composed of middle- and upper-middle-class women who embraced an elite view of literary study. The oral component of the meetings was vital in the clubs' aim to foster the education expected of women belonging to these classes. Activities such as pronouncing quotations at roll call and reading the plays aloud highlight the importance of elocution. The West Side Shakespeare Club even appointed a club critic whose role was to correct the women

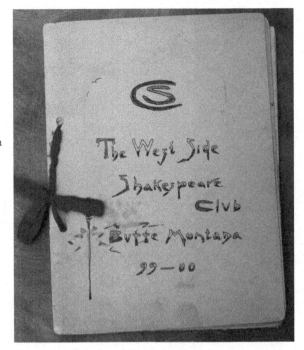

Figure 14. West Side Shakespeare Club program from 1899 to 1900. The women from this Butte club produced the booklet for the year's course of study, hand-drew the cover, and bound it with red ribbons. Program is in the Butte-Silver Bow archives. Photo by Kevin Brustuen, 2017.

who were not pronouncing words properly.[15] Shakespearean language seemed an ideal subject for elocution, thus his words became the standard by which frontier women measured their ability to sound as if they were still in the eastern United States.

Programs from these literary clubs attest to an array of material related to Shakespeare, fostering a deep engagement with his entire canon and an understanding of historical and contextual information.[16] The Dillon Shakespeare Club passed on their books to the public library, where they remain to this day as a testimony to the range of scholarship that the women were consulting alongside their reading of Shakespeare. Some of the works are A. C. Bradley's classic, *Shakespearean Tragedy*, Marchette Chute's *Shakespeare of London*, and George Brandes's *William Shakespeare: A Critical Study*, but the library is extensive, including an impressive array of historical material that aided these women in their research and paper-writing.[17] These books show every sign of having been heavily used, including passages that are underlined and marginal notations that indicate the depth of engagement with this scholarly material.[18]

The Present and Its Politics

Despite the historical orientation of this library, the women's interests were not confined to the past. In fact, consistently they sought ways to make links between Shakespeare and current events. Even club mottoes show this aim; the West Side Shakespeare Club's Latin motto, "*Tempore parendem*," admonishes them to "be prepared for life," and the bylaws state the club's objective as "the mutual improvement of its members in literature, art, and science and the vital interests of the day." In a similar vein, turn-of-the-century Deer Lodge annual programs show an interest in topics as diverse as ladies in literature, the eccentricities of William Shakespeare, the soaping of the geysers in Yellowstone National Park, the Punic Wars, and the question of marriage. Relevance was never far from these women's minds, thus they were eager to make links between Shakespeare's history plays and contemporaneous events as they paid attention to the tensions in Europe on the eve of World War I. When these clubs participated in relief efforts for the soldiers, it was not a departure from their engagement with literature but a continuation of it.

Club programs, minutes books, and histories provide a wealth of information about the study topics that most interested Montana women at the turn of the twentieth century—topics that suggest an active attempt to relate Shakespeare to their own situations. Although some clubs did include single and even working women, most members were married women who were undoubtedly reading Shakespearean texts through the lens of their experience as wives and mothers. Not surprisingly, therefore, several clubs examined characters such as *King John*'s Constance "as woman and mother."[19] Flora McNulty of Virginia City extended this interest to Shakespeare's biography as well, writing:

> Mary Arden, Shakespeare's mother, was of gentle birth and wealthy. Her ancestors are traced back not only to the Normans but to the Anglo-Saxons. She brought culture and refinement into her husband's family. She was an ideal Mother and became the Storehouse from which the great dramatist in after-years drew material for his matchless pictures of women.[20]

"Culture" and "refinement" are the operative words here, for, as Katherine Scheil suggests, in such outposts Shakespeare often became "part of the civilizing process."[21] For the women of Montana, however, being civilized wasn't the whole story—one also had to be strong, which was an attribute that they sought in Shakespeare's female characters as well. An essay about Desdemona from a West Side Shakespeare Club member was printed in the newspaper in 1902, arguing stridently that for "all her timid flexibility and soft acquiescence" she is not weak, for "the mere presence of goodness and affection implies in itself a species of power, power without consciousness, power without effort, power with repose, that soul of grace."[22] This interpretation points to an important facet of the Montana woman's identity in this period, which involved marrying the strength required to live in this unsettled place with a dignity and poise that were expected of women in the time period.

As the club programs attest, the women were hungry for models in Shakespeare's characters that could help them to explore different types of femininity. Featured discussion topics included the women of *Hamlet*, the girlhood of Lady Macbeth, Shakespeare's ideal woman, laws affecting women, and the strength of Shakespeare's women.[23] The questions the women posed tell us even more: "Which is the truest wife? Catherine, Hermione, or Lady Macbeth?"[24]; "Is it Apparent in Act I, that the Love of Desdemona and Othello holds within itself the Promise of a Violent Future?"; and "Is Hermione more highly developed than other of Shakespeare's suspected wives?"[25] The West Side Shakespeare Club discussed "Beatrice's test of Benedick as it appeals to the modern woman,"[26] which provocatively sets the stage for how these women related Shakespeare to their own concerns. Unfortunately, we are left with far more questions than answers, for the minutes books almost never provide any details about how the club members responded to these prompts. Thus, when the minutes of this club record that "the members discussed Claudio's treatment of Hero most seriously and earnestly,"[27] we can only imagine what the women thought and said about the young man in *Much Ado about Nothing* who slanders his bride on their wedding day and leaves her at the altar. The serious and earnest discussion, however, surely included strenuous objections to Claudio's behavior by these self-described "modern women."

In addition to studying the works of their namesake, Shakespearean clubs also frequently engaged with contemporary literature. For instance, in the early years of the twentieth century, several clubs were discussing and even seeing productions of Henrik Ibsen's *A Doll's House*.[28] This play, which caused both outrage and excitement when it premiered in 1879, dared to show a woman leaving her oppressive life, walking out on her husband and children.[29] The Yellowstone Club of Livingston even had the opportunity to meet with the actress who played Nora in *A Doll's House* the afternoon before her performance and "went home enthused and induced [their] husbands and friends to go to the performance in the evening."[30] Undoubtedly characters such as Hero, Hermione, and Desdemona were measured against the example of Nora in these women's minds.

When considering Shakespeare's female characters, the women could consult various sources, as the Dillon women did. Their resources included a book entitled *Heroines of Shakespeare*, as well as Charles Wingate's *Shakespeare's Heroines on the Stage*. The opportunity to see and learn from the actresses who embodied such heroines on the stages of Montana was not lost on the club women. Missoula took great pride in being chosen as a stop on Ellen Terry's lecture/performance tour in December of 1910—the only stop, the newspapers were quick to point out, between Spokane and St. Paul.[31] Terry was one of the most famous actresses of her day; she was a British star who had become known for her performances of Portia, Beatrice, Lady Macbeth, and many others. By 1910 she was sixty-three years old, and she was regarded as a legend of the stage who knew everything about Shakespeare's women. This particular lecture was arranged as part of the University of Montana, and in the weeks leading up to the event the newspapers reported on, and created, a great deal of enthusiasm. She was said to be an incomparable impersonator and "a Shakespearean woman incarnate."[32] Special train service was arranged to and from the neighboring town of Hamilton to accommodate the anticipated crowds that came to her lecture at the Harnois Theatre. At that time the *Missoulian* ran an article in which Terry was asked whether Beatrice from *Much Ado about Nothing* would have been a suffragist if she had been alive now, and Terry's answer was that "Beatrice, Rosalind, Portia would all be suffragists," for "the question of women's rights is not new."[33]

Women's suffrage gained support much earlier in the intermountain West than it did in many other parts of the country; Wyoming was the first state to grant women the right to vote, and Montana elected the first female to congress. This representative, Jeannette Rankin, was invited by the Dillon

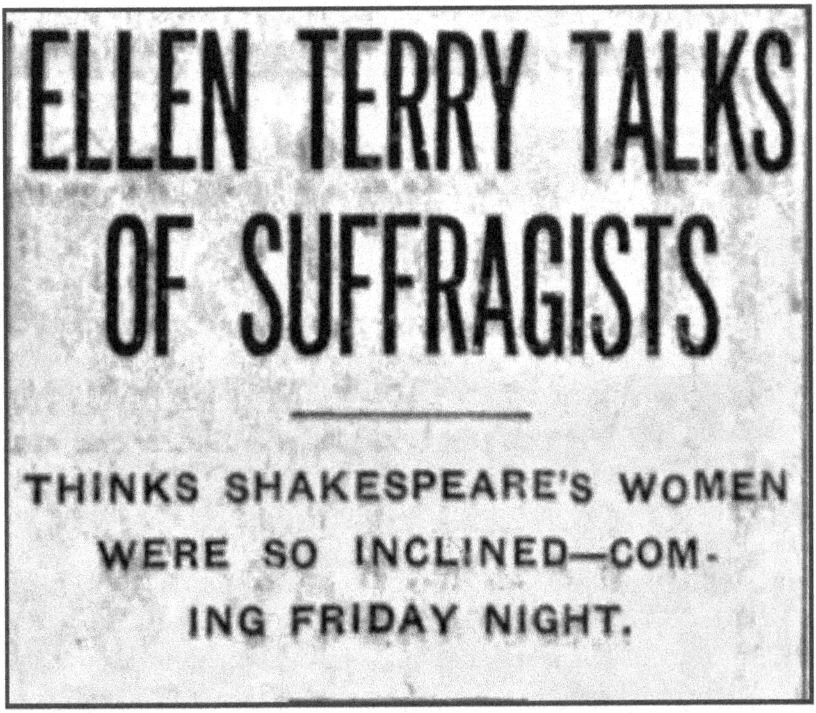

ELLEN TERRY TALKS OF SUFFRAGISTS

THINKS SHAKESPEARE'S WOMEN WERE SO INCLINED—COMING FRIDAY NIGHT.

Figure 15. A headline from *The Missoulian* (December 14, 1910) about Ellen Terry's visit to Missoula, during which she talked about the links between Shakespeare's heroines and women's suffrage.

Shakespeare Club to speak about women's suffrage in 1912,[34] and she spoke in Livingston at the Montana Federation of Women's Clubs convention in 1913. The event was hosted by the Yellowstone Woman's Club, which had been reading and discussing Shakespeare since its inception. One woman from Missoula who attended the convention, Mary Bandmann, epitomizes the links between women's suffrage and Shakespeare in Montana. Mary was an actress and the widow of the well-known German actor Daniel Bandmann, who had settled on a ranch in Hellgate Canyon (see chapter 4). After her husband's death in 1905, Mary raised four children, headed the Shakespearean division of the Missoula Woman's Club,[35] performed at local functions (especially the "seven ages" speech from *As You Like It* [2.7.140–67] and the letter scene from

Macbeth [1.5.1–54]), directed high school plays, organized benefit performances for the indigenous children at the St. Ignatius mission, presented at the horticultural society, and, not incidentally, ran the ranch.

Mary Bandmann's biography is instructive, for it gives a window into the many roles that Montana's women undertook in this period; they were involved in multifaceted activities and responsibilities of daily life, which meant that their time in the women's clubs was both an extension of the work and a much-needed respite. Bandmann made a guest appearance for the Hamilton Woman's Club, entertaining them by performing selections from Shakespeare, but the minutes book records an interesting detail that was articulated that night: "Our President expressed the sentiment of all when she said 'we had all worked hard and were tired and this couple hours of Entertainment was what we needed.'"[36] This comment points to the women's consistent hard work in their varied roles, which was bound to lead to their desire for concomitant rights.

In 1906, one of the women in Mary Bandmann's Shakespeare division presented a paper on "the women of Shakespeare," and another about "the needed reform in time-honored customs," making it clear that the women were making links between the suffrage movement and Shakespeare's portrayal of female characters. Richard van Orman posits that women in clubs of this period who were "involved with women's suffrage used certain lines from the Bard's plays and from his virtuous women like Portia and Cordelia to strengthen their appeal for the vote."[37] We have no concrete evidence that Mary Bandmann did so, but we do know that in 1913 she attended the meeting of the Women's Federated Clubs in Livingston and stayed on to hear Jeannette Rankin speak at the suffragist convention. By 1915, Jeannette Rankin was giving regular lectures on suffrage in the University of Montana library in Bandmann's hometown, and the voice of Shakespeare's outspoken heroine Beatrice can almost be heard in the background.

Playing Shakespeare

A frequent activity for the early women's clubs was reading aloud. Much of their engagement with Shakespeare's plays began with assigning parts and reading through them in their entirety—a practice that was both physical and communal.[38] From this foundation it was a natural step to expand into semipublic entertainments and performances, with women offering their own interpretations of Shakespeare's drama.

Extensive records about the Fortnightly Club of Helena survive, but no remnant is more striking than the two beautiful watercolor portraits that depict the women of this club performing Shakespeare (see figures 16a and 16b). One shows two women talking conspiratorially, under which is written a line from *The Merry Wives of Windsor:* "Why this is the very same" (2.1.73). In the other, the clown Touchstone from *As You Like It* is dressed in motley, with a quotation from the play handwritten below: "It is ten o'clock. Thus may we see, quoth he, how the world wags" (2.7.23). Above each picture are the names of the actresses who played these roles. This careful artwork shows the pride and delight these women took in performing Shakespeare in full costume, taking on the roles that included not just female characters similar to themselves but clowns, princes, and villains. The attraction of impersonating is apparent in an account of women from Great Falls putting on a production of *A Midsummer Night's Dream* (see interlude 1). One woman begged to play Hermia's part, for "Didn't Hermia have two lovers? How exciting for an over-worked housewife!" So diligent was this aspiring actress that she wrote her lines on sheets of paper that she pinned to her sleeves so she could practice her part while attending to the housework.[39]

The women of Dillon were especially invested in a production of *Merchant of Venice* that they put together in 1902 in order to raise funds to build a club-house. They performed the full-length play in the Dillon Theatre and spared no expense in making it a notable event; they even rented elegant costumes of silk, satin, velvet, and broadcloth from a Salt Lake company. The advertising and build-up of the event were successful, for within two hours of the box office opening, over two hundred seats were sold.[40] After the performance, the newspapers abounded with praise for the production, especially the skilled performances by these amateurs. One review complimented the "charm" of each character, including "Shylock's plea on behalf of his own selfish and evil ends," while another commended the actor's "great dramatic skill in her dig-nified and sympathetic rendering of the much wronged Jew. Her interpreta-tion of this often misunderstood character revealed a man of strong passions and keen intellect whose nature had been warped and distorted by bitter persecution. [She] showed unusual power in rendering this difficult role."[41] This description cuts against many popular nineteenth-century portrayals of Shylock as a comic villain, for it takes his plight seriously and considers the

Figures 16a and 16b.
Watercolors depicting two
Shakespeare performances
by the Fortnightly Women's
Club of Helena. The
paintings are at the Montana
Historical Research Center.
Photos by Kevin Brustuen,
2008. 16a) Two women
portray Mistress Ford and
Mistress Page in *The Merry
Wives of Windsor*, with a
line from the play written
below and an actress's name
(Mrs. Turner) above. 16b) A
woman identified as Mrs.
Leslie portrays Touchstone
from *As You Like It*, with a
line from the play written
below.

sociological problems that created this hate-filled character. The nuances of this empathetic portrayal no doubt arose as a natural outgrowth of the club's frequent study and discussion of *Merchant of Venice* in the previous years.

The Dillon women were known not only for their public performances but also for their annual entertainments, to which they invited their husbands as well as club women from neighboring communities. In 1899, Mrs. Christie of the Homer Club in Butte traveled to Dillon for a celebration featuring *A Midsummer Night's Dream*, which included instrumental and vocal solos, abridged scenes entitled "The Complaint of Egeus" and "The Mechanics Planning Their Play," and a tableau representing Lysander and Hermia. Guests then enjoyed a meal where all of the courses were accompanied by an appropriate quotation from Shakespeare: "The boar will use us kindly" (*Richard III*, 3.2.32) for the ham, "I have not slept one wink" (*Cymbeline*, 3.4.100) for the coffee, "Such lack of kindly warmth?" (*Timon of Athens*, 2.2.217) for the ice cream, and even "Here's a dish I like not: / I cannot endure my lady Tongue" (*Much Ado about Nothing*, 2.1.252) for this unexpected appetizer.[42] The event's merriment included a series of toasts. The most impressive was given by Mr. Jones, whose witty speech was reprinted in the *Anaconda Standard*. He appealed to the "Mistress of the Feast":

> Yet "full of vexations come I with complaint," and, speaking for my un-
> happy sex, this, the "glorious summer" of your festal day, but marks the very
> "winter of our discontent." What our grievances? Legion! But first, we of
> the proscribed sex come here in the innocence of our trusting hearts, un-
> armed; and how are we met? Why, every one of you has a club! . . . I do not
> care if the constitution does guarantee to citizens the right to bear arms; it
> was never intended that women should be allowed to have clubs.

Jones's mock horror continues with the dangers of allowing women education, which can result only in reforms that are detrimental to their men, who will be cowed by the "clubs." Yet the upshot is clear, in the words that Jones adapts from *Othello*: "Oh, excellent wretch! Perdition catch our souls, but we do love her, and when we love her not, chaos is come again."[43]

A similar good-natured war of the sexes was evident in an event sponsored by the Billings Women's Club in 1904. The women performed multiple scenes from *Macbeth* and *As You Like It* for a mixed audience. The newspaper praised the event and the accomplishment of the women: "Tragedy and comedy were enacted at Elks' hall last Friday evening and some of the best known and dearest characters created by the Bard of Avon issued forth from between their covers and briefly stalked the boards." The festivities afterward continued under the complete direction of these female Shakespeare enthusiasts. The husbands were put in their place: "The men were not expected to do very much and they did not disappoint their hostesses in that regard. They were overwhelmed by the mental alertness and intellectuality of their wives and were glad to be permitted to be there!"[44]

If the war between the sexes was one recurring motif underlying these occasions, the war with nature was another. The narration of the 1899 Dillon celebration is juxtaposed with the physical conditions of life in Montana: "Saturday morning the storm clouds hovered near and . . . burst into a blinding snow storm; but a storm was a little thing to the visiting club women after the cordial welcome of the evening before."[45] The downpour that caused an abrupt ending to the Great Falls women's outdoor production of *A Midsummer Night's Dream* (see interlude 1) also points to the physical vagaries of weather. Yet in both cases, the storm did not undo the success of the event, because it was a part of the natural environment they sought to evoke. The Great Falls women arranged to perform in a field that they termed a "marvelous convenient place"; participants rode upon a hay wagon to a large field, where these "housewives in lacy muslin" had prepared to perform a full rendition of the comedy.[46] Like the women of Dillon, the Great Falls club members sought inspiration from the play for the luncheon menu that would accompany the performance: the split pea soup and meat and mustard sandwiches deliberately evoked the fairies named Peaseblossom and Mustardseed. Given the full engagement with the plants and food that come from nature, as well as the open-field setting, the production of Shakespeare's woodland comedy lost nothing when the storm came—in fact, such a turn in the event added to the story of its success. Scheil notes that, in many frontier clubs, Shakespeare is seen "as the apex of intellectual achievement even in adverse conditions."[47] In this case, however, the Shakespearean event capitalizes on the discomforts of the physical environment. As Charlie Russell admitted in his rendering of the Great Falls event, "All's Well that Ends Well" (see Figure 7).[48]

Alongside these amateur theatricals, the women's clubs consistently studied professional actors and their portrayals of Shakespeare's plays. Many clubs took a particular interest in Maude Adams, the actress from Salt Lake City who became an international sensation for her portrayal of Peter Pan. Heber Wells, governor of Utah, compared her to "one of the great silver or lead or copper mines that abound in this region—we walk all around it every day for perhaps a generation, never realizing that a hidden treasure lies at our door, and then some bright day a David Belasco or some other Napoleon swoops down upon us, is attracted by the formation, discovers the mine, and develops it."[49] Long before she was Peter Pan, however, Adams played many of the heroines in Shakespeare's plays, including Juliet, Viola, Rosalind, and Portia. She passed through Montana in 1912, but even when she was far away the Montana newspapers followed her and reported on her successes. In 1912 the Fortnightly Club of Helena was discussing Adams's portrayal of Rosalind in open-air productions around the country. Just as the women felt drawn to perform in their physical environment, they were fascinated by actresses who were carrying on that important historical aspect of Shakespearean performance.

Continuations

The literary focus of these Montana clubs was more prominent in their first decades. By the dawn of World War I there were more diverse focal points, such as civic engagement, relief efforts for soldiers, the building of parks, and scholarship funds for girls. Despite its name, the Dillon Shakespeare Club moved from their initial focus on British literature to cover other topics, such as women's suffrage, prohibition, and civil service reform; similarly, the As You Like It Club took up the question "Should marriage laws be revised?" and read an article entitled "The Unquiet Sex," which argued that women's clubs are different from men's, because "instead of being a place for recreation they are only another place for hard work."[50] The *work* of the reading groups and the *work* of women on the frontier—whether it be ranching, teaching, home-making, or building a society that could counteract the threatening forces of the Wild West—was something that united these women in a shared sense of purpose. As a result, the women became increasingly confident of their own contributions to society. Their ideas were also no longer confined to local meetings, for they could share thoughts by writing in the *Montana Woman*, a monthly publication by the Montana Federation of Women's Clubs. This magazine enabled women across the state to share literary, educational, and political viewpoints. On a regular basis Shakespeare references cropped up in relation to more contemporary issues. Reflecting on the Teapot Dome bribery scandal in 1927, an article in the *Montana Woman* likened the situation to the witches' cauldron in *Macbeth*.[51] The article opens by citing the "venomous slime and sickening odor" of the upheaval, with an extended quotation of "Round about the cauldron go . . . "[52] The parallels are cleverly and expertly drawn, illustrating a dual understanding of classical literature and contemporary politics.

That very same year the West Side Shakespeare Club raised a considerable sum to sponsor a lecture from Columbia University professor and Shakespeare scholar John Erskine. In his memoir *To the Memory of Certain Persons*, Erskine describes in humorous terms the process of arriving in Butte and being asked "whether I preferred a he-man's day or a quiet session with the Ladies' Sewing Circle." He chose the former, which began with highballs and tours of the mines, followed by more drinking and piano playing, until "a sobering thought occurred; I had come to Butte to give a lecture!" Erskine showed up in a bit of a haze, and describes the evening thus:

> My lecture at Butte had been arranged by the Literary Society of the town, a group of ladies who probably were accustomed to the ways of their men-folk. Throughout the day the members of the program committee had been receiving bulletins of my progress, and when I appeared at the lecture hall they showed—as it seemed to me—signs of relief. They knew I would be there, but they hadn't been sure in what condition. So far as I could see, they were satisfied, or even pleased, by my platform performance. Beyond question the audience was hugely entertained, not necessarily by what I said, but by the cooperation I had from my loyal hosts, the mine managers. If accidentally I lifted an eye or an eyebrow, they took it as a signal that I had said something witty, and a laugh should be forthcoming. After each rousing guffaw I found myself making a hasty attempt at something funny, so that the hilarity might have an excuse, even if belated.

In the end he admits that "they were an amazing group, apparently with unlimited reserves of endurance, but as soon as the train drew out, I crawled into

Figure 17. Copper-covered program from the West Side Shakespeare Club, 1936–1937. The material chosen for this annual program is appropriate, considering the importance of the copper mining industry to Butte. Program is in the Butte-Silver Bow archives. Photo by Kevin Brustuen, 2017.

my berth and fell asleep."[53] In the written history of the West Side Shakespeare Club, the event sounds much more serious and edifying:

> At different times over the years the Club was able to bring superior speakers before the group, and the appearance of John Erskine, noted lecturer, was sponsored by Shakespeare Club. This was done at the cost of three hundred dollars, which in itself was an accomplishment since the treasury was a very modest one. Mr. Erskine was more than worth what it cost in time and effort.[54]

The contrast between the flippancy of Erskine and the seriousness of the West Side Shakespeare Club is striking. Erskine might have dismissed them as eccentric and amusingly provincial ladies, but the women themselves were quite adamant about what they wanted to gain from such lectures. Even if a male presenter behaved badly, they were determined to use this occasion to learn something about Shakespeare that justified the work bringing him to Butte had entailed.

There is a remarkable continuity to the activities of club women across Montana, though the choices they made, from club mottos and curricula to the nature of their annual entertainments, show that they were not merely following a single prescription for literary clubs. In a unique choice that epitomizes the West Side Shakespeare Club's connection to the mining industry of Butte, their annual programs for 1936 and 1937 have a thin copper cover (see figure 17). This particularity, though, is balanced by the breadth that the women gained through their studies. As one Dillon woman put it:

> The wide range of subjects treated [in Shakespeare] has deepened our understanding of people in varied environments, living under varied circumstances with varied background and opportunities, or lack of opportunity, living in other countries and in other times. Our sympathies have been broadened and our tolerance increased.[55]

The engagement with Shakespeare shows the ways in which they strove for self-education that was both historically grounded and relevant to contemporary political issues. The Helena Woman's Club motto was taken from Shakespeare's contemporary, Thomas Heywood: "The world's a theatre, the earth a stage, which God and Nature do with actors fill."[56] This saying is apt for the women's clubs throughout the state, for it shows that these Montana women recognized that they were on a stage—a huge stage on which they acted out a complex intersection between politics, literary study, and life in a quickly changing world. In many respects these women's clubs echo the concerns and structures of other clubs across the United States, but they had a distinctive quality too, caused by the strong push toward women's emancipation in the West and an awareness that the study of literature, especially Shakespeare, would always be grounded in the physical environment of work as well as recreation. These Montana women studied Shakespeare's words but also played with them, boldly taking on the roles that suited them best.

INTERLUDE 3
ANNIVERSARY CELEBRATIONS

> Let's talk of graves, of worms, and epitaphs.
>
> —*Richard II*

On March 4, 1916, an article in the *Daily Missoulian* was headlined, "Whole World to Commemorate 300th Anniversary of Shakespeare's Death." The report was that "in practically every large city of the country there are to be during this year community plays, masques, festivals, pageants, tableaux, and other forms of celebration," whereas in smaller towns the celebration would come "in the form of special study courses, club programs calling for essays on Shakespeare, and in many other ways." In that year there were indeed worldwide celebrations for the Shakespeare tercentenary, and Montana's citizens organized their own events as part of the global acknowledgement of this towering literary figure. The state university in Missoula replaced its spring convocation ceremony with a special Shakespearean program featuring lectures by professors, a series of Shakespeare songs, and scenes from the plays acted out by the drama students.[1] All events took place outside, in front of the library, and concluded with the planting of a Shakespeare tree; such a symbolic act assured that the commemoration of the event, like Shakespeare's works themselves, would live on for subsequent generations. Western Montana College likewise celebrated Shakespeare in Dillon, involving not just the university community but the active women of the Shakespeare Club.

The state's largest tercentenary celebration was undoubtedly the one in Butte. It came about through the initiative of Mrs. James Floyd Denison, who approached the mayor with the idea to coordinate a series of commemorative events. The mayor and several aldermen formed a committee and worked alongside Mrs. Denison and others to organize what was a truly impressive municipal effort. A series of lectures was given with the aim to "familiarize the public with the simple greatness of the writer, of his many-sided yet accurate views of life's different phases and interests, of his common interest in and sympathy with all classes and all conditions."[2] A special program on April 26 featured scenes from *Julius Caesar*, *Hamlet*, and *Merchant of Venice*, performed in elaborate costumes ordered from the East Coast. All events were accompanied by extensive musical programs—vocal, orchestral, and dance (including "16 of the city's prettiest young women," who danced the Elizabethan garland dance).[3] Meanwhile, the women's clubs organized their own functions in conjunction with this municipal tercentenary. Mrs. Denison herself gave a "studio lecture" at her home, speaking about *Cymbeline's* Imogen as the most perfect female character. The newspapers covered every event, glorying in exalted language about Shakespeare. No praise, it seemed, could be too great: "In literature Shakespeare is the great arc light, against which all others are incandescent, or flickering tallow dips. He is the central sun around which thousands of planets or stars of lesser magnitude radiate only a pale reflecting light."[4]

The religious communities were also not to be left out of such commemoration. One lecturer was Rabbi Wittenberg, whose presentation was about Shylock; and with conviction for the spiritual importance of these observations, the committee organizing the tercentenary urged "every pastor to bring in his Sunday morning sermon on April 23, some appropriate remarks or references to the great poet."[5] Tapping into the commercial side of the celebration, Victor Records ran a newspaper ad in honor of the Shakespeare tercentenary, proclaiming that "the songs of Shakespeare are now, for the first time, available to all" through a series of records that preserve "the long-forgotten music of Shakespeare" in "a permanent memorial to the great poet and dramatist."[6] The songs included "Under the Greenwood Tree" from *As You Like It* (2.5.1–7) and "Tell Me, Where Is Fancy Bred" from *Merchant of Venice* (3.2.63), as well as an air sung by Ophelia, and many others.[7] These twin poles—the religious and the commercial—show a great deal about the appeal of these 1916 celebrations. The three-hundred-year anniversary was an occasion to celebrate and reflect on why Shakespeare mattered in the early twentieth century. To this end, memorialization was the central focus, whether that meant looking back several centuries or embracing a technology of the future that could make Shakespeare immortal.

The communities of Butte and Anaconda worked hard to make sure that children also played a part in the tercentenary. Students from Butte High School and from St. Joseph's High School performed their own scenes from Shakespeare, while the children of the Paul Clark Home (an orphanage for disadvantaged children[8]) had their own little celebration, in which they recited quotations from Shakespeare, told stories from the play, and had a contest to see how many words they could form from the word "Shakespeare."[9] The Butte High School paper published a feature about one of their new students, Charles Matthews, for it seemed appropriate in the midst of the tercentenary celebrations to learn more about this boy's father, who had spent the first fourteen years of his life in Stratford-upon-Avon. Mr. Matthews attended a village school, read parts of *The Tempest*, stole fruit from Warwickshire orchards, and carved his initials into Anne Hathaway's cottage, but the most memorable feature of Stratford was the landscape: "Charles' frequent references to the beauty of the quaint old English hamlet showed that the father has especially impressed that idea upon his son's mind. 'Such beautiful scenery is enough to inspire one to write great poetry,' said he." The article concludes with an implied question: "Just what effect such ancestral environment may have upon Charles, the reporters, being insufficiently acquainted with him, are unable to foretell."[10] Shakespeare's past and Mr. Matthews's past are recollected in this piece in order to include Montana in the worldwide celebrations of 1916 but also to make the important point that such histories should have a positive impact upon the future of the region and its people.

Although the events in Butte were certainly the most elaborate, other schools across the state also decided not to let the tercentenary go uncelebrated. The Glasgow High School in the northeastern corner of the state put on a performance of *Taming of the Shrew* to honor the anniversary, daring to stage what was at that time a lesser-known play. The newspaper gave a thorough synopsis of the plot for those unfamiliar with *Taming of the Shrew*, calling it a "laugh-provoking play" and joking that "every married man and prospective husband in Glasgow should be on hand to see how it is done."[11]

The Catholic Ursuline Academy in Great Falls was even more ambitious, for they designed a tercentenary celebration in the form of a Shakespeare pageant and ball. The young women presented a huge array of characters, sang, danced, and performed masques. In the most memorable masque, "The witches performed some magic passes and soon conjured up the shade of Shakespeare, who recognized his own creations, graciously introduced them to Queen Elizabeth, and the rest of the company."[12] Such celebrations focused on the splendor that could be achieved through Shakespeare—the power of the young actors who delivered their lines with believability, who donned lavish costumes, who sang and played Shakespearean songs along the way. What is most noticeable, in fact, is the sheer expansiveness of these Shakespearean presentations, available to young voices in all regions.[13]

All of these tercentenary celebrations indicate a desire to showcase the community's education, talent, and vibrancy. The grand results of Butte's civic celebration were presented at a meeting of the Drama League in St. Louis. The *Butte Miner* expressed excitement about how this would promote Butte not just as a mining town but as one that participated in a full-scale artistic commemoration of a great author.[14] By 1916, the people of Montana no longer felt on the margins of civilization, especially as Butte had taken center stage in the production of copper for the war effort, but they wanted to assert their cosmopolitan nature as well. Participation in a global cultural movement demonstrated that Butte was more than just its mining industry. At the same time, it is significant that even those smaller communities like Glasgow made sure that their voices would be part of the worldwide chorus praising Shakespeare. No town or state was too out of the way to appreciate the author who was ceaselessly lauded as the most universal.

One hundred years later, at a time when the praise of Shakespeare really could be global, people around the world once again mounted a series of events to commemorate the landmark anniversary of his death. In London, a year-long celebration entitled "Shakespeare400" was organized to connect public performances, musical and art programs, exhibitions, and creative activities in the capital and beyond, and similar activities were taking place in dozens of countries worldwide.[15] Montana's contributions to these events in the spring of 2016 were centered in the two university towns. The Folger Shakespeare Library in Washington, D.C., sent a First Folio to one location in each state as part of the 2016 celebrations, and Missoula was chosen as the

Montana location. The University of Montana's Mansfield Library displayed the First Folio for a month and organized lectures and workshops for teachers and students in conjunction with this anniversary year, organized under the banner "First Folio! The Book That Gave Us Shakespeare."

In Bozeman, the quatercentenary celebration sought to combine university and civic voices. Mayor Carson Taylor proclaimed April 23, 2016, as "Shakespeare Day." He read the proclamation before the city commission, which included the clauses "Whereas Shakespeare's works have had enduring impact upon our language, history, and culture throughout the world, the United States, and Montana," and "Whereas Shakespeare continues to be a key figure in our educational system, our arts organizations, and our communities." On April 23, MSU students and faculty, as well as actors and citizens from Gallatin Valley, presented a series of flash mob performances from Shakespeare, while lectures and performances took place at downtown Bozeman's independent bookstore, the Country Bookshelf, throughout the day. Shakespeare's words gained an unexpected currency as Henry V's St. Crispin's Day speech was used to inspire crowds at the Co-op, Richard III wooed Lady Anne at Wild Joe's coffee shop, the clown Launce from *Two Gentlemen of Verona* appeared with a real dog at the Bent Lens optical store, and children performed scenes from *Twelfth Night* in the lobby of Bozeman's first hotel, the Baxter. A century after the Butte tercentenary, Shakespeare was celebrated, and memorialized, in Montana once again. No matter which anniversary is observed, such commemorations give Montanans a way to become part of a global phenomenon, while also insisting upon the uniqueness of their local Shakespearean culture.

TRAVELERS AND SETTLERS
OF THE THEATRE

I have watched and traveled hard.
Some time I shall sleep out, the rest I'll whistle.

—*King Lear*

In 1875, a young Irishman named John Maguire arrived in Montana Territory's Fort Benton via steamboat, with a letter of recommendation from General George Custer in hand. Maguire went to the fledgling town of Butte, which had a population of only three hundred people; there, in a newly built but empty store, he performed a one-man show consisting of recitations and songs that highlighted his Irish brogue.[1] Like Laura Honey Agnes Stevenson (see chapter 2), Maguire found appreciative audiences in mining towns such as Pioneer, Philipsburg, and Louisville. Maguire was an experienced actor, but his vision was entrepreneurial; he knew show business because his cousin Tom was a successful theatre manager in California, and he also carefully followed the career of California theatre producer David Belasco.[2] John Maguire spent the next thirty years as a theatrical impresario, creating and managing performing arts spaces in western Montana that housed the most popular entertainers of the day.[3]

When he was a young actor, Maguire had the privilege to perform with Lawrence Barrett (himself the son of Irish immigrants), playing minor roles opposite Barrett's Hamlet, Macbeth, Petruchio, and Romeo. From that time forth Maguire idolized Barrett, thus it was with great pride that he brought the celebrated actor to the fast-growing mining towns of Butte and Helena in 1884 to present *Hamlet, Merchant of Venice*, and Bulwer-Lytton's *Richelieu*. Maguire charged double the standard ticket price for this unprecedented event, but no one seemed to complain. The *Helena Weekly Herald* noted that Barrett "will be worth seeing in his wonderful characters that can be seen in Helena only once in a life-time, and never but once in the mountains."[4] Such an event was a symbol of the growth and development of western Montana up to this point but also a forerunner of what was to come. By the century's end, Butte was one of the premier stops for major touring artists and companies in the West—a reality that began with Maguire's vision in a tiny town in 1875.

An extraordinary range of Shakespearean actors came through Montana between 1885 and 1925. The cultural center was Butte, but rarely did entertainers pass up the opportunity to perform before audiences in other venues across the state. The majority of the star Shakespearean actors in the nineteenth century were from Europe, thus Montana received visits from the English Ellen Terry, the French Sarah Bernhardt, and the Polish Helena Modjeska. Such an array of origins was especially appropriate to Butte, a thoroughly polyglot town. Audiences were mesmerized by the women of the stage. Although Modjeska was an immigrant who had only recently learned English by the time she first came to Montana, her portrayal of Rosalind delighted because she was "beautiful in person, natural in manner, . . . the ideal of Shakespeare's masterly creation."[5] Montana's most prolonged love affairs with actors, though, centered upon two European-born men—Daniel Bandmann and Frederick Warde—who appear more often in reports and folklore about Shakespeare in Montana at the turn of the twentieth century than any others.

Daniel Bandmann: Settling in Montana

Daniel Bandmann's story is a romantic one, especially from a nineteenth-century perspective. He was born in Germany in 1837, came to the United States as a teenager, and acted in German-language productions in New York.[6] After being tutored in English by the young Alexander Graham Bell, Bandmann made it on the American stage more broadly. He traveled far and wide, not just throughout America and Europe but to Australia, India, China, and Hawaii—a journey on which he reflects in his grandly titled book *Seventy Thousand Miles with Shakespeare*. Bandmann was one of the many

Figure 18. Helena Modjeska as Rosalind in *As You Like It*, circa 1893. This Polish-born actress made several trips to Montana to perform Shakespeare in the 1890s and 1910s. Prints and Photographs Collection, Library of Congress, LC-USZ62–77307.

itinerant actors who came to Montana in the 1880s, but when he arrived in Butte in 1884, he was hailed as "the biggest theatrical attraction that ever visited Montana."[7] On this tour he played Hamlet and Shylock, and the responses were enthusiastic. Herr Bandmann was unquestionably "the great tragedian," an epithet that nearly always accompanied references to him in the newspapers.

What separates Bandmann's story from those of other itinerant actors is that he decided to buy land in Montana and settle there. Although he never completely gave up the theatre—returning to New York to act occasionally, giving frequent readings in Montana, and running an informal acting school—he was essentially, from 1887 to his death in 1905, a ranch man. He bought 320 acres in Hellgate Canyon, on which he raised cattle, sheep, chickens, and apples.

The idea that an internationally known actor would choose the life of a Montana rancher feeds into myths of the West. Newspapers throughout the state freely told his story, reporting on the exotic cattle he bought, as well as his adventures and misadventures on the frontier. Nowhere is the story told more colorfully, however, than by Bandmann himself. In 1902 he reflected upon the decision he made fifteen years earlier:

> I was willing to give up the living of a metropolitan life to the trying struggles, the uncertain results and vicissitudes of a Montana rancher in those days. I was willing and anxious to invest the money I had made as an actor in stock and help to develop and live in a state which will be one of the grandest countries in the world.

Bandmann acknowledged his lack of knowledge, but he certainly did not lack enthusiasm: "I knew nothing of stock, but I loved it. I knew nothing of poultry, but I loved it. I knew nothing of pigs, but—yes, I loved them, too—they always seemed to me so much like my fellowmen, full of greed, greed, greed, and was not I greedy, too? Didn't I want land, and lots of it?"[8] Such self-awareness was one of his charms: he made it clear that his desire to own land was a sort of avarice, but one that was an acceptable, even laudable, ambition on the frontier. At the same time, Bandmann's tale about his first performance in Missoula is infused with humorous anecdotes about the primitive conditions of this new town. He and his company were featured at the opening of John Maguire's opera house in Missoula,[9] but Bandmann noted that this venue was really an old livery stable that had been turned into a "thespian temple," which was ultimately built on top of a manure pile:

> When the ghost descended through the trap door, the smell of well-rotten manure of two or three years' standing, that greeted my nostrils was so terrible that I might have exclaimed with Falstaff, "That it was the most damnable putrid and offensive odor," sufficient to knock a man down and to gather up enough poesy to finish the act.

The actor playing the ghost quit after the first night because of the putrid smell, and the entire cast was soaked from traipsing back and forth between the theatre and the home that served as their dressing room. Nonetheless, Bandmann had to admit that, although "there was hardly a decent looking house among the shanties that made up the town," he "played before a most intelligent and enthusiastic audience" that was surprisingly broad and metropolitan, and therefore his stay was enjoyable.[10]

Always one to tell his story with abundant Shakespearean references woven into his language, Bandmann explained that when he was on tour in Canada and received word of a deal he could make on a cattle ranch in Montana he "nearly jumped out of [his] 'gabardine' for joy,'" for he was dressed as Shylock at the time.[11] Bandmann's story is woven together with Shylock's more often than any other—not just by himself in his "Jewish gabardine" but because of an identification between his history and the part for which he was most famous. The implicit connection between Bandmann and this role no doubt owed something not just to his acting skill but to his own origin as a German Jew. On his first visit to Montana in 1884, Bandmann and his troupe made special appearances in Helena and Butte where they presented plays in German—both Schiller's *The Robbers* and Act 3 of *Hamlet*, which were sponsored by the Hebrew Benevolent Society. Perhaps Bandmann's foreignness contributed to the portraits of his eccentric behavior. Sometimes legendary stories were told about Bandmann insulting others or getting himself into legal battles, or about his taking stage sword-fighting skills a bit too seriously, or about a good-natured bet that he could climb to the summit of Missoula's Mount Sentinel and back in two hours (a wager he easily won).[12] Yet even in the midst of such accounts, the lighthearted toleration of this Hellgate Canyon resident is infused with his ubiquitous identity as a Shakespearean actor.

One legend tells of Bandmann's dealing with a group of Flathead peoples who camped on his land, refused to pay for the toll bridge he had established over the Clark Fork River on his land, and who were, he thought, killing and eating his prized chickens. He dressed in a mélange of acting garb, including a black silk stovepipe hat, a red wig, a waxed moustache, false eyebrows, and assorted colors of clothing. Much to the Native peoples' surprise, "He began to dramatize parts from Shakespeare. He went from one language to another as his gestures added emphasis, and his eyes would pop and squint beneath the cleverly arranged false eyebrows. The Indians lost their serene smiles of indifference as the performance took on loudness. . . . They were spellbound." They quickly packed up and left, and Bandmann declared that "words have saved my kingdom, where the shotgun would have failed."[13] We have no way of knowing whether some version of this event happened, but the circulation of this anecdote speaks to Bandmann's eccentricities, to his ubiquitous

Figure 19. Daniel Bandmann as Shylock in *The Merchant of Venice*, circa 1863. Both before and after he settled in Hellgate Canyon, Bandmann was most famous for his portrayal of this character. University of Washington Libraries, Special Collections, UW37026.

association with Shakespeare, and to an attitude whereby "ignorant Indians" are driven off the land by a histrionic multilingual performance.[14]

Bandmann became fully integrated into Missoula's community through building a toll bridge, actively participating in the horticultural society, introducing McIntosh apples to Montana, and encouraging the start of the University of Montana theatre program.[15] At the same time, though, he haunted the theatrical scene both spiritually and literally. One story reported in the *Anaconda Standard* in 1900 told of an itinerant troupe that came to Missoula's leaky opera house. The grumbling actors had to dress in tiny rooms and the stage was lighted by kerosene lamps serving as primitive footlights. Yet when the curtain opened the actors were inspired, because among the audience of cattlemen and miners in the front row sat a rough-looking bearded man, who was none other than Daniel Bandmann.[16] Bandmann's obituary in the *New York Times* printed a version of this story, narrating that the New York actors were delighted to see this legend, "a grim, shaggy-haired, stern-browed old man" who "made it a point to go behind the scenes and talk about old times with the players who happened to drift to the far-away Montana village."[17]

Bandmann understood his own life in Shakespearean terms, weaving famous quotations into his account: "'Many a time and oft' have I been asked: How is it that you departed from your vocation as an actor and took to that of a rancher and stockraiser in Montana?" He immediately thinks of *As You Like It* and the retreat to the Edenic woods, articulating in romantic terms that "during my whole life as an artist my soul was always directed towards nature and the love of beautiful and useful animals."[18] An 1899 newspaper article on Bandmann featured his seemingly unlikely turn from actor to rancher, equating it with his famed performance as Jekyll and Hyde on Broadway:

> From the stage to the orchard; from the theater to the farm—it is a long distance as measured by habits and by customs, but the change has been made, apparently with ease, by Herr Bandmann, and he has brought to his Montana farm the zest and energy that were characteristics of his work upon the stage.[19]

Repeatedly Shakespeare's position vis-à-vis nature is overlaid with Bandmann's story, giving license and imaginative weight to this unlikely biography.

Such associations took a bitter turn when Bandmann's personal life was criticized by the newspapers in 1892. He impregnated and then married the young California actress Mary Kelly, only to be accused by his British-based actress wife Millicent Palmer of committing bigamy, and by his long-term acting partner and associate Louise Beaudet of not sharing his company's proceeds from their international tour. The scathing article about Kelly's attempt to escape to Spokane and hide her and her child's identity painted Bandmann in the most damning terms. Tellingly, the story's author weaves together agricultural and Shakespearean references, giving full measure to the dual public opinion about this famed immigrant, who is dubbed the "actor-rancher, the histrionic Hamlet, the plain, every-day despoiler of virtue." The title of the article declares: "It is a Holstein: Mary Kelly's identity established beyond a doubt," and the author promises the whole truth, quoting from *Richard III* that "an honest tale speeds best, being plainly told" (4.4.358). Mary Kelly is portrayed as the victim of this famous man, who overpowers her with his fame and promises. As an innocent wide-eyed actor, she is lured to take lessons at his ranch and "she consented, believing his protestations, trusting his honor, and above all thinking that here of all places, in the heart of the mountains, in the home of the muses and the dwelling place of poetry, she could best continue her studies for the stage."[20] The author imagines them reading sonnets, interspersed with *Venus and Adonis* and the *Rape of Lucrece*. Returning to *Richard III*, the article concludes that Bandmann should likewise have a conscience with "a thousand several tongues, each one condemning him for a villain" (5.3.193–95).

For a time the illegitimate child and the charges of bigamy caused a scandal, especially when Bandmann's former partner, Louise Beaudet, who also seems to have gone by "Mrs. Daniel Bandmann," sued the famous actor and managed to succeed in acquiring some of the capital that she insisted (no doubt correctly) was hers. Outrage toward Bandmann and his newest wife (Mary Kelly) did not last, however. Within a short period of time the scandal blew over, the required divorce certificates were produced, and the newspaper coverage returned to praise for the local celebrity, who occasionally left Montana in order to perform on the East Coast and in Europe. Mary continued to act and to be involved in the Missoula Woman's Club (see chapter 3). Throughout the 1890s she and Daniel gave frequent performances in western Montana, touring to Butte, Anaconda, and Hamilton with an amateur dramatic society from Missoula, with themselves taking the parts of Shylock and Portia in *Merchant of Venice*. The settlement of the Bandmanns in Montana serves as an apt metaphor for a changing theatrical culture in the state, as theatres were built that provided a permanent home for Shakespeare and those who made his works come to life.

Frederick Warde: Traveling Montana

When the actor Frederick Warde first came to Butte in 1891 to play the title role in Shakespeare's *Henry VIII*, he arrived with a letter of introduction from an entrepreneur in San Francisco, which he presented to Marcus Daly, the "copper king" of Butte. As Warde wrote in his autobiography, "The result was a very cordial welcome and an opportunity to see everything of interest in the camp, our experience including a descent to the 800-foot level in the celebrated Anaconda copper mine."[21] This tour led him to the heart of Butte: the massive underground network of tunnels where the majority of the workforce spent their days. Unlike the ghost of Hamlet's father (whom Hamlet describes as an "old mole" who "work[s] i' th' earth so fast"[22]), Warde subsequently remained aboveground, becoming an honorary citizen of Butte because of his frequent trips there.

In his autobiography, Warde fondly remembers his numerous dealings with the witty John Maguire, whom he called "a man of many eccentricities, generous to a fault, loyal to his friends, fond of good company and ready to recite at every opportunity."[23] Maguire's resourcefulness was epitomized in Warde's account of a time that he was to play King Lear, but the newspaper did not have a picture of the actor to run for the advertising. Not deterred, Maguire instead pulled a newspaper cut from a play about an Italian teenager and ran it as an ad for Warde's play, with the caption "King Lear When a Boy." Warde wrote, "I recognized John's ingenuity, and had a hearty laugh, but when we met protested that King Lear could never have looked like that. The only satisfaction I got was, 'Well, who's to prove it, my bhoy?'"[24]

Even though he was excited and eager about the opportunities in Montana, Warde was liable to complain about the primitive conditions, just as Bandmann had during his first appearance in Missoula. When Warde performed at the Bozeman Opera House, he gave a curtain speech expressing dismay that the dressing room ceilings were only five and a half feet high and annoyance that the stage roof was not raised enough to permit the use of modern scenery. As a result of this speech, Bozeman's Committee on Public Buildings voted to repair and remodel the opera house, including the addition of a special room to store scenery.[25] The attention to scenery and set pieces in the 1890s shows the importance of large, lavish productions in this period. Gone were the days when solo actors could come with just a few props, for now the fashion was to delight audiences with panoramic backdrops, huge casts, and special effects that strove for historical representations of the periods depicted.

Joint-stock companies formed to manage theatrical business, promoting the most famous actors and booking their national tours. Warde's appearances were always connected to this kind of theatrical endeavor; sometimes he ran his own company and other times traveled under the auspices of another. He appeared alongside other stars of the day, none more frequently than Louis James. The *Great Falls Tribune* opined, "Since the famous Booth–Barrett organization there has been no attraction that has created such a universal sensation in the theatrical world as the Frederick Warde and Louis James combination."[26] When they appeared together in 1895 Bandmann came to the Butte performances, showing an appreciation for these theatrical colleagues and congratulating Maguire on his continually growing theatrical empire. By 1899 Warde and James were joined by Kathryn Kidder and managed by Wagenhals and Kemper. This triumvirate of actors played repeatedly in Montana, delighting audiences with *Othello*, *Hamlet*, *Macbeth*, and Sheridan's *The School for Scandal*. Their company consisted of thirty-two people, and their productions were impressively large in every way.

The Warde-James-Kidder rendition of *Othello* was especially acclaimed by the reviewers, one of whom wrote, "It is a thing long conceded that James is the best Othello and Warde the best Iago of this generation, if not of all time." Repeated curtain calls and ovations expressed audience enthusiasm for what they regarded as a perfect rendering of the tragedy. Appreciation for character was in large part determined by appearance, thus James was "a splendid looking Othello, keen, resourceful, broad chested, and above all in any pose he is picturesque." Opposite such a star as James, portraying Iago required a complexity at which Warde excelled: "It requires a fine and cultivated intelligence to interpret that most despicable role. . . . His work is so strong, subtle and telling that no one could ask a better actor in the role. . . . He is absolute sovereign of dramatic art."[27] Warde went on to play the role of Othello many other times in his career, investing the part with a pathos that he considered crucial for the character and his tragedy. When he performed, Warde demanded the audience's proper attention and respect. One night he played Othello, but when he "stooped to kiss Desdemona before he plunged the dagger into her heart, someone in the audience or gallery made a smacking noise simultaneously with the kiss." An outraged Warde ordered the curtain to be put down and "called the person who made the noise a blackguard" because he had made what should have been sublimely sorrowful instead ridiculous.[28] In addition to insight about Warde's personality, this newspaper account also gives clues about what version of *Othello* was performed on this occasion. In Shakespeare's play Othello smothers Desdemona, but a staging

Figure 20. The famous acting duo of Frederick Warde and Louis James, who performed regularly in Montana in the 1890s, gained particular fame as Iago and Othello. Warde traveled more extensively through Montana than any actor during the end of the nineteenth and beginning of the twentieth centuries. Prints and Photographs Collection, Library of Congress, POS-TH-POR.W374, no. 1.

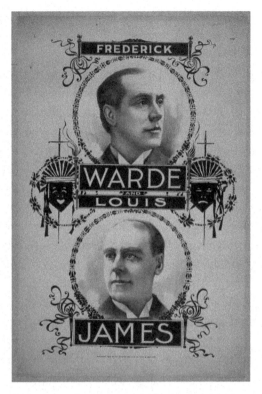

wherein she is stabbed is characteristic of some popular nineteenth-century bowdlerized versions.[29]

Many productions of this period showcased the talent of the actors in tragic roles—thus Bandmann was "the great tragedian" and Warde was best known for playing in *Othello, Julius Caesar,* and *Macbeth.* There was also a place for Shakespeare's lighter plays at the turn of the century, though some of the most notable comic productions were featured not just in opera houses but also in scenic outdoor locations. In September of 1900, a production of *A Midsummer Night's Dream* starring Louis James and Kathryn Kidder, with a company of forty-one people, drew 2,500 spectators in the Columbia Gardens amphitheater. Columbia Gardens, an amusement park, was given to the town in 1899 by mining mogul William Clark, who owned the electric street cars that transported the citizens to this oasis. Columbia Gardens provided an array of attractions, including a carousel, a horse-racing track, a small zoo, a beer hall, and a wooden roller coaster. It was also, not surprisingly, a site for large outdoor entertainments—lavish productions featuring huge panoramas and period costumes. The scenic splendor of the *A Midsummer Night's Dream* production was notable, and many remarked on the representation of dawn at the end of Act 4, which was accomplished by "an elaborate system of transparencies, electrical color lights, gorgeous columns and moving panoramas."[30] A similarly lavish production of *As You Like It* the previous month also took advantage of electric footlights; one reviewer remarked with approval that "the entire stage was brilliantly lighted and presented a most beautiful appearance."[31] The technology for lighting these productions of Shakespeare was, of course, directly connected to Edison's economical delivery of electric current through copper wires. At this time, at least half of the copper wires that supplied the United States with electricity originated in Butte, and the citizens were duly proud of this fact. That thousands of spectators witnessed the miracle of electricity by watching a Shakespeare play shows a great deal about just how common it was to see these plays in turn-of-the-century Butte.[32] Responding to the demand for transportation to these performances, the street railroad company arranged for extra trains to shuttle Butte's residents to and from Columbia Gardens.[33]

By the time James and Kidder were performing at Columbia Gardens, Warde was seen more often in the lecture hall than he was on the stage. He appeared in myriad locations—in the theatres, the high school auditoriums, the Elks Club, and at women's club events. Warde spoke at a reception sponsored by the West Side Shakespeare Club, which was described as "one of the most brilliant social functions ever witnessed in Butte."[34] A newspaper report of one Elks gathering wryly commented that when such occasions are announced the men, but especially the women, flock to it: "To hear Warde speak, to hear the elocutionary efforts of others, . . . drink the delicious punch and claret cup, what could woman want more?"[35] Warde was no doubt charismatic and a living testimony to what he preached in his lectures: a thorough understanding of Shakespeare made one witty, charming, eloquent, and morally sound. Shakespeare, Warde insisted, was true to nature, and thus he sought to bring this truth to his audiences—both those in the theatre and those in the lecture hall.

Warde lived longer than many of his contemporaries and was still acting

Figure 21. The lovers from *A Midsummer Night's Dream* in an outdoor production at Butte's Columbia Gardens in 1900. The production starred Louis James and Kathryn Kidder and drew 2,500 spectators.

long after Maguire, Bandmann, Modjeska, and others were gone. As a perpetually itinerant actor, he traveled widely, treating audiences in isolated communities to his Shakespearean appearances. In 1911 he played Brutus in a production of *Julius Caesar* in Glendive, which was announced as one of the greatest events in the history of their opera house. The Glendive newspaper wrote:

> It rests with such scholars as Warde to keep burning the spark of genius to tell us that in the past there was a better and brighter day. . . . In this day, when people cheaply pleased are being lured from real merit in the drama to pernicious and perverted plays, it is a merciful godsend to the real lovers of the drama to find a player with the courage of his convictions, who faces the onsweeping wave of tawdry inconsistency in the theatre and upholds high standards and high ideals because they are noble and beautiful and beneficent.[36]

As this report shows, Warde was viewed as a relic of a glorious past who epitomized the dual role of the actor and the lecturer. His legacy was that he always managed to convey a heightened sense of morality through his engagement with Shakespeare.

The Circuit: Shakespearean Lectures

Warde's appearances as a public speaker and Shakespearean expert were not unique, for other actors also moved into a lecturing role, such as Ellen Terry and Augustine Dwyer, and these alternative performances were popular and well-attended. Such actors traveled solo, giving impersonations, monologues, and lectures about Shakespeare. More often, though, the lecturers weren't actors but instead educators or religious leaders who used Shakespeare to express their principles. Dr. Eisenberg of Butte was a rabbi, a lecturer, and a mining prospector all rolled into one, and he always gravitated to Shakespeare. When he spoke to a gathering of Jewish people in the wake of President McKinley's assassination, Eisenberg took on his natural role as an orator: "I am forced to exclaim with Mark Antony over the body of Brutus: 'This was the noblest Roman of them all.' His life was gentle, and the elements so mixed in him that nature might stand up and say to all the world, 'This was a man.'"[37] As Shakespeare's *Julius Caesar* itself proves, the influence of an orator cannot be underestimated. Traveling speakers in nineteenth-century America were often part of the Chautauqua circuit, an adult education movement that sought to bring culture and entertainment to rural communities. Regardless of their affiliation, lecturers who taught elocution ranged widely in order to reach audiences across Montana and made a living by entertaining, teaching, and moralizing with Shakespeare.

The superintendent of Helena schools, R. G. Young, gave a speech about *Othello* in 1894 that excited a great deal of negative criticism. Young went against the prevailing view of his day, which was to praise Shakespeare and his protagonists effusively; instead, he suggested that Othello was written during a time of notorious immorality in England, so the play reflects its own period. Young thought the relationship between Othello and Desdemona was vulgar and read Othello not as heroic but as an "imp of Satan, defective in manner and lacking in principle, a black, low-born knave." John Maguire was horrified when Young gave this speech in Butte and responded with a scathing editorial, countering that Shakespeare is "the Morning Star, and guide and pioneer of true philosophy," both a product of a beautiful period in history and its chief spokesman. For Maguire, there were not multiple ways to look at Othello's character: he was a noble Moor descended from the conquerors of Spain, not an "uncivilized African." Maguire quipped that Young was liable to imagine Othello deciding against suicide, then going off to "some Venetian Dakota for 90 days' residence." In the end, Maguire's reaction was so strong that he said Young was unfit to place his views before the young people of Butte.[38]

Daniel Bandmann, not one to keep silent when it comes to interpretations of Shakespeare, also entered the fray. He was so offended by Young's views on *Othello* that he challenged him to a duel that could determine whether the "lecture is a true sentiment or a profanation."[39] The people of Young's native Helena remained a bit more loyal to him in this matter, saying that Bandmann lost his temper. However, when Young continued his lecture circuit by giving the speech in Miles City, it was greeted with similar ire—how dare he call Othello a brute and Desdemona a wanton! The criticism directed at Young attests to high stakes when it came to interpreting Shakespeare; the plays were not just about entertainment, for they were used as exemplars of moral truth. To suggest anything impure or immoral in Shakespeare meant to go against the author who was just one step away from Holy Writ.

Another kind of educator who gave lectures on Shakespeare was the elocutionist. One of the best known was a Montana native named Mabel M. Gormley (the "M," in fact, stands for Montana), who was born in Alder Gulch, educated in Michigan, taught in several states, and returned to Montana, eventually settling in Great Falls.[40] In extensive tour circuits throughout the state, she used Shakespeare to teach elocution and the Delsarte declamation method. Gormley was known for her "esthetic drills and statue poses" as she performed scenes such as Lady Macbeth's sleepwalking monologue. This kind of entertainment was widely appreciated; the *Great Falls Tribune* praised her 1901 performance, saying that "her facial expressions are eloquent" and "her pose and gestures would tell the story to a foreigner unacquainted with the language."[41] Her stylized approach to Shakespeare shows a connection to educational movements of the day, too, for it emphasized storytelling through gesture, statue poses, and set pieces designed to showcase declamatory power. Even though this is worlds away from the natural acting styles to which we have become accustomed, what Gormley demonstrated in her lecture was in keeping with what audiences saw when Shakespeare was performed on the stage in her day: Louis James was likewise noted for his "statuesque proportions" and "grand voice" when he performed the role of Othello.

Given the emphasis on education, elocution, and high moral principles in Shakespeare lectures, we might wonder whether the entertainers were ever also humorous. Reports of the solo shows by the English actor, lecturer, and humorist Ben Scovell make it clear that he frequently had his audiences roaring with laughter, but even so, his aims were deeply connected to a moral agenda. In fact, Scovell's usual performance venue was the local Methodist Episcopal Church. Scovell had a history that fascinated his audiences, probably because it was more legend than truth. Reports claimed he was the nephew of the famous actor Henry Irving, but a contrasting biography claimed he was a penniless orphan who was sent to Toronto for a time, then tried his hand as a cowboy in Texas before proceeding to study at Harvard and the American Academy of Dramatic Arts, even winning the competitive Belasco scholarship. Whatever path he did take, however, we know that Scovell went to the Boer War and entertained the Canadian troops (where he met Rudyard Kipling). Scovell continued his work as an entertainer for the troops in WWI, and his postwar shows were designed with the same sort of line between uplifting poetry and spiritual truth, on one hand, and palliative laughter, on the other.

During his 1922 tour of Montana, Scovell performed in Methodist churches in Great Falls, Helena, Butte, Anaconda, and Missoula. His repertoire included several Shakespearean bits, such as the ducat scene from *Merchant of Venice*, the downfall scene from *Henry VIII*, and the quarrel scene from *Julius Caesar*. These more serious Shakespearean pieces were usually followed by some farce or comedy that Scovell had written himself, and the balance invariably left audiences satisfied. Scovell sometimes filled pulpits along the way, serving a role as an entertainer-preacher-actor and continuing to speak to war veterans and other citizens in communities across Montana.

Not Quite Dead: Shakespeare's Silver Age

The Ballad of Buster Scruggs is a 2018 film by the Coen brothers that contains six vignettes about life on the American frontier. In one of these, entitled "Meal Ticket," a theatrical impresario travels by wagon throughout the Rocky Mountain West, making money by featuring a young man with no arms and legs who recites monologues from Percy Bysshe Shelley, the Bible, and Shakespeare. At first audience members are numerous and the one-man show makes enough money to support the duo, but after times become too difficult the impresario changes his tactic by buying a chicken that can supposedly do math problems and throwing the trunk-only actor over a bridge. As is typical of the Coen brothers, this sardonic story is darkly funny but also poignant. The recitation of Shakespeare's Sonnet 29 emphasizes the vignette's portrayal of loss and hardship: this melancholy itinerant actor "beweep[s] [his] outcast state" with cries that are "bootless" in more ways than one.[42]

The great impresario John Maguire died in 1902 in Monterey, California, and his tombstone, made of Montana granite, bears the epitaph: "Ring down the drop- / Life's fitful play is o'er." The latter line is a close echo of a line from *Macbeth* that served as the headnote for Maguire's eulogy to Lawrence Barrett: "After life's fitful fever, he sleeps well" (3.2.24). The sense of closure and nostalgia expressed in these words wasn't just about the passing of a generation of actors. Could it be that after the turn of the century Shakespeare was also dying in Montana?

The actors who still performed Shakespeare in the twentieth century began to seem like has-beens whose time to ride into the sunset had come. Thus, the Butte paper said of Helena Modjeska in 1902: "She's been a good old wagon, but she's done broke down." The reviewer reflected, "Occasionally, flashes of her old-time fire lit up the piece," but even so, "Madame Modjeska's performance gave Butte people the impression that she should be satisfied with the glory she has won and take her future satisfaction from her triumphant past."[43] During her farewell tour a few years later, audiences were more kind to Modjeska, and Billings in particular was thrilled to witness her famous rendition of Lady Macbeth. That was the last time Montana audiences saw the Polish superstar, with the possible exception of a film that appeared in 1908, allowing her ghostly image to be viewed once again. The Billings paper announced that the Orpheum Theater would be showing several short films, including *Macbeth* starring Modjeska, which would be "one of the finest pieces ever shown on an animated picture screen."[44] No record of such a film survives, but even if this was a misadvertisement, it does echo a crucial historical shift from stage to screen.

Montana's newspapers published enthusiastic ads about Shakespearean films and spectacular stars who made the roles come alive (even before the technology enabled words to be part of the experience).[45] Frederick Warde was always eager to place himself before audiences, so he embraced the opportunity to be in the earliest Shakespeare films. He starred as Richard III in a 1912 rendition of the play that is the oldest known complete feature film made in the United States. This silent *Richard III* begins with a metatheatrical frame: Warde is in modern dress, emerges from behind a curtain, and bows before transforming into the medieval king. In addition to dominating the screen in this version, Warde lectured at screenings and read excerpts from Shakespeare's play while the reels were changed.[46]

Because of Montana's remoteness, the opera houses often lacked live entertainment, so the new medium allowed them to bring audiences together on a more regular basis. Invariably, however, this development made live performances less tenable. Femme fatale silent film star Theda Bara never set foot in Montana, but she appeared on screens throughout the state. The Sexton Theatre in Great Falls, which was designed not for live productions but for film, proudly showed William Fox's *Romeo and Juliet* in 1916, and the newspaper hailed the star, Bara, as "the foremost actress of the screen."[47] When Bara's *Cleopatra* film was shown in Glasgow, the paper noted, "It is now playing all the larger cities and it is only to break the long rail road jump that the Orpheum was able to book it at all at this time."[48] A few decades earlier the actors themselves had appeared in small towns like Glasgow, but now it was only the reels that came to these remote areas.

The 1920s saw major growth and development of the film industry. The lavish displays, massive casts, and histrionic gestures of silent film were occasionally used for portraying Shakespeare, but much more often other subjects were taken up. The biggest hit of that decade was *Queen of Sheba* (1921). Quick to point out a local connection to Hollywood, Montana papers repeatedly reported that Daniel Bandmann's widow, Mary, was playing the role of Bathsheba in this epic picture. This turned out to be false information, but it reflected the desires of Montanans to see their own performers on the silver screen. Nevertheless, the actor who played Solomon in the *Queen of Sheba* film, Fritz Leiber, was in fact the most popular actor-lecturer to tour Montana during that decade. He had played Mercutio in a silent film version of *Romeo and Juliet* (1916), but Leiber had a great deal to *speak* to his Montana audiences when he took his 1923 tour of Great Falls, Helena, Butte, and Missoula. His performances were hailed as wonderful and moving, but the newspapers reflected something that would have seemed foreign a generation earlier: assurances that these Shakespearean plays were accessible. A Great Falls editorial read:

Those who failed to see and hear Fritz Leiber and his company in Shake-speare's tragedy, "Hamlet," at the Grand theater Wednesday night because they expected it to be uninteresting and "over their heads," little realize the opportunity they missed of witnessing a play as fascinating and diverting as any of Broadway's latest dramas.[49]

Promoting the relevance of Shakespeare to his audiences, Leiber interacted with young people in particular. In Great Falls, he had a luncheon with the high school basketball team and a group of sixth grade boys. He gave readings from Shakespeare and talked about the import of his works, despite the pas-sage of three centuries, reading from *Hamlet*, *As You Like It*, and *Merchant of Venice*.[50] As Leiber continued his tour in Missoula, he was lauded for attempt-ing to connect to his audiences through Shakespeare: "In these days of leg shows, picture shows and jazz shows it requires a special kind of courage to re-introduce Shakespeare to the public with the hope of arousing interest."[51] He was praised for his presentation of *Taming of the Shrew* and *Hamlet* to the people of Missoula, which "was an intellectual feast for the students, teachers and townspeople of our university city." A nostalgic review of Leiber's perfor-mance reflected upon the heyday of Shakespeare in this town's theatres:

Time was when Shakespeare was known and appreciated in Missoula.
Thirty years ago such sterling actors as Louis James, Frederick Warde and
Robert Mantell played Shakespeare in three-night engagements in the few
cities of Montana. Then there was our own friend and neighbor, Daniel
Bandmann, a distinguished actor of international renown.[52]

This 1923 review captures the sense that there was a golden age of Shakespear-ean acting in Montana, when the country's most renowned stars would tread the boards of opera houses around the state. Those days had passed, though, and Shakespeare's future in Montana would look decidedly different.

INTERLUDE 4
THE MARGINS

Haply, for I am black
And have not those soft parts of conversation
That chamberers have . . .
—*Othello*

Shakespeare has all too often been assumed to speak for a dominant, white, bourgeois ideology. Montana's story sometimes supports such a view; it cannot be denied, for example, that the majority of the women's reading groups in Butte consisted of the middle and upper classes, who met in dwellings owned by the families of the mining companies' management, not their workers.

Would Shakespeare always be on the side of the oppressors in labor struggles? When Montana writer Ivan Doig entitled his 2013 novel *Sweet Thunder* and set it in 1920s Butte, he took the opposite view. The main character, Morrie Morgan, is a schoolteacher, librarian, and journalist who writes editorials for a socialist newspaper that attacks the Anaconda Copper Mining Company. Morrie names the newspaper *Sweet Thunder*—a phrase taken from *A Midsummer Night's Dream* (4.1.117) and meant to evoke a revolutionary voice in support of the labor strikes.[1] Throughout the novel the wisdom of Shakespeare, symbolized by his bust in the Butte public library, is aligned with a Marxist ideal that strives for the liberation of the working classes.

Having Shakespeare speak for the oppressed minority is not only a product of the twenty-first-century novelist's imagination, however, for the newspapers in Plentywood, Montana, in 1919 give historical precedent for this approach. During this period Shakespearean quotations were frequently evoked in order to support the political views of the editorialists. The wronged farmers, for instance, were encouraged to remember that "thrice is he armed who hath his quarrel just" (a quotation from *2 Henry VI*, 3.2.233).[2] A similar editorial speaks out against class distinction and lambasts the hypocrisy that assumes "violence to maintain conservatism is all right, whereas preaching violence as a means of reform is all wrong." As a sort of warning, the writer co-opts a line from *Romeo and Juliet*: "If conservatism by violence rules, we may expect in the words of Shakespeare 'these violent delights' to 'have violent ends.'"[3]

Justice and law were the main concerns of these socialists, who sought reassurance that the situation would improve. The line "The law hath not been dead, though it hath slept" from *Measure for Measure* (2.2.91) provided the basis for one editorial that cried out against the injustices of the past:

> The worst of laws is the law which some men can put to sleep part of the time—the law that sleps [*sic*] while one steals a million and is wide-awake to pounce on the man who steals something to eat, or the law that searches the laboring man's speech for violence and is dead to the talk of gunmen ... and tar and feather up-stairs.[4]

That the quotation is taken out of context (in Shakespeare's play it is spoken by the hypocritical Angelo, who uses law for his own ends) is hardly unusual. People on every part of the political and religious spectrum have always quoted Shakespeare's words in support of their views, as they have the Bible. For Montana's one "red corner" in the early twentieth century, on the margin both politically and geographically, Shakespeare provided a font of wisdom that both inspired and assured.

This voice from a small community in the northeast corner of Montana encourages us to think of other histories, other peoples whose story is less often told. The population of African Americans in Montana, for instance, is rich with history and culture, especially in Virginia City, Great Falls, Helena, Billings, and White Sulphur Springs. The women in these communities, like their European-descended contemporaries, also formed clubs. Overall their focus was more often civic improvement and occupational skills, but some also had literary aspirations: the Afro-American Woman's Club in Butte formed a Shakespeare Department, as did the analogous Billings Club.[5] These clubs were linked to the socially active African Methodist Episcopal (AME) churches, which sponsored lectures and performances all over the state. None of these garnered more attention than the visit that the famed educator Booker T. Washington made to Butte, Bozeman, and Helena in 1913. Black and white audiences alike attended his popular lectures, as well as the receptions that followed at the AME churches. We don't know whether Washington spoke about Shakespeare in his Montana lecture, but we do know that he often did so. *Othello* is a natural choice for the voice of emancipation, but Washington used the play in a somewhat unexpected way, noting that "slavery exemplified Othello's plan—'Put out the light'—put out the light of liberty and then put out the light of intelligence."[6] Washington's worry was that, like Othello, his fellow African Americans lost their faculties of reason when they were enslaved, which caused them to behave barbarously.

Ultimately, however, Washington was concerned more with the future than the past for African Americans, and to this end he found Brutus's words in *Julius Caesar* apt:

There is a tide in the affairs of men
Which, taken at the flood, leads on to fortune;
Omitted, all the voyage of their life
Is bound in shallows and in miseries.[7]

In essence, then, Washington drew upon Shakespeare both to explain oppression and to express a hope for a coming age in which the situation could and would improve. The philosophy of these lines spoke volumes to Washington and his followers: people must watch for the moment in history when they can further their own cause.

During the early twentieth century, Montana's women were manifestly interested in questions of race, as attested by the activities of the women's reading groups. In 1911 the *Anaconda Standard* ran the usual report about what the women's clubs were discussing. The West Side Shakespeare Club was taking up issues related to *Othello*, and the Atlas Club was discussing "prominent colored men" such as Booker T. Washington and Paul Laurence Dunbar. These adjacent reports cry out for a connection between the racial politics of Shakespeare's play and those of early twentieth-century America, but there is no specific evidence that the women discussed this relationship.[8] For the African American women's groups, however, a stronger connection between Shakespeare and racial politics is evident. The secretary of the Dunbar Art and Study Club in Great Falls wrote "Booker T. Washington" on the cover of the club's 1922 ledger book.[9] One otherwise blank page in this ledger has "Shakespeare" written at the top, followed by lines from a poem that rewords Washington's favorite passage from *Julius Caesar*, but after that the record discontinues.[10] Such ledgers necessarily provide an incomplete picture of these women's political discussions about the place of African Americans in Montana during this interwar period. We know what they liked to quote but not what they said or thought about these quotations. Yet even a meager record such as this testifies to Shakespeare's inclusion in the discussion. Just allowing the words to speak for themselves, in fact, seems to have been an important part of Shakespearean encounters in the 1920s. An impersonator and actress named Eva B. Walker, who formed a dramatic club in Minneapolis-St. Paul under the auspices of the NAACP, performed scenes from *Othello* and *Merchant of Venice*, but there is no way of discerning her attitude toward the racial and ethnic charge of these plays. Walker's 1922 tour of Montana, sponsored jointly by the NAACP and the AME churches, took her to Billings and Great Falls. She was a versatile artist, for her program featured passages from *Merchant of Venice* but also a recitation of Robert Service's "The Spell of the Yukon." The latter poem is about a miner who is driven to despair by the vagaries of this life yet remains transfixed by the beautiful landscape that surrounds him.

In the 1890s, the mining town of White Sulphur Springs was not forlorn but instead a bustling community with an active performing arts scene. In 1892 there was a debut performance of the Amateur Dramatic Company, and the Colored Folks' Cornet Band performed overtures before each of the two main events: selected scenes from *Merchant of Venice* and the popular ballad opera *The Bohemian Girl*.[11] These events testify to a mixing of different races, classes, and kinds of entertainment in one community. African American and white performers appeared together, and the material ranged from minstrel shows to recitations and staged debates. One historian writes that "an African American performer who could flawlessly recite a speech from Shakespeare

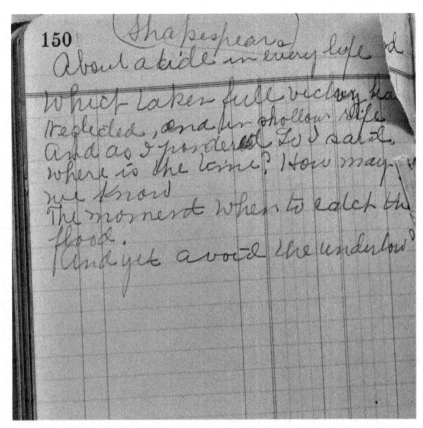

Figure 22. A ledger book from the Dunbar Art and Study Club of Great Falls, 1922. The club secretary has written "Shakespeare" at the top of the page, followed by words derived from a *Julius Caesar* speech that Booker T. Washington often quoted. "Booker T. Washington" is also written on the cover of this book. The ledger book is at the Montana Historical Research Center archives. Photo by Kevin Brustuen, 2018.

as well as speak in the fractured dialect associated with minstrelsy would at least call into question the widely-held assumption that such dialect was not a put-on but a natural and realistic representation of black speech."[12] This is a provocative position, for it is difficult to imagine the same performer "putting on" black dialect and moments later performing Shakespeare. Nonetheless, it seems likely that this is exactly what happened in White Sulphur Springs.

Engagement with Shakespeare was never as strong as the excitement for musical groups in White Sulphur Springs. The town produced several black performing artists of national fame, but none of them was known for performing Shakespeare. Taylor Gordon, White Sulphur Springs' most famous celebrity, was born in 1893 and wrote in his biography, *Born to Be*, of the advantages of coming of age in this small Montana town.[13] He performed music regularly as he was growing up there, then became a well-known singer and vaudeville performer in New York during the Harlem Renaissance. Throughout his performance career, however, Gordon shied completely away from Shakespeare.

In contrast, Montana's most well-known black film actor, Jess Lee Brooks, who was born less than a year after Gordon, had a thorough engagement with Shakespeare throughout his life. Brooks grew up in Great Falls and Helena and was known for singing, recitations, and performing in a wide array of plays. In 1937 he was in two stage productions in Los Angeles: in *Merchant of Venice* he played the Prince of Morocco, and he performed the title role in an all-black production of *Macbeth* that was based on Orson Welles's New York production. This particular adaptation was set in "dark, moody Africa"[14]; as one reviewer put it, this allowed "for the introduction of weird dance ensembles and jungle chants."[15] Such a "blacking" of the Scottish play smacks of racial stereotypes today, but in the 1930s, in a production that employed seventy African American actors, it was part of taking ownership of Shakespeare and telling the story from a marginalized perspective.

Brooks's most notable film role was as a preacher in *Sullivan's Travels*, in which he sang a stirring rendition of "Go Down Moses."[16] He was not himself destined to be a Moses character leading his people into newfound freedom, but Brooks was from his earliest days a political thinker who was deeply concerned about the plight of African Americans in the West. When he was sixteen years old (in 1910), Brooks wrote a column for the Great Falls High School journal, *Round Up*, entitled "Race Problem in the West," which was reprinted in the Helena newspaper, *Montana Plaindealer*. Brooks wrote passionately:

> Is it jealously [*sic*] that makes you hate us and persecute us so? Or is it because of our black skin? Surely if you are a Christian, you know we all came from one family. . . . Can you not see that we are bound to develop?

Figure 23. Jess Lee Brooks as Macbeth and Mae Turner as Lady Macbeth in the 1937 production at the Mayan Theatre in Los Angeles. Jess Lee Brooks grew up in Great Falls and Helena but went on to have a successful stage and film career. Federal Theatre Project digital collections, Library of Congress, Image 22 of Production Notebook.

. . . Education is what is making and is going to continue to make us a great people. What we must have are highly educated leaders. . . . Lazy, restless negroes are immigrating from the south and coming north and the majority of the black population in small western cities are of this type. Fifty per cent of them can neither read nor write and they only make the struggle harder for honest negroes.[17]

As Anthony Wood points out, this speech is a deliberate corrective to the industrial education championed by Booker T. Washington. When Brooks speaks of the desire for highly educated leaders, the return to classical texts such as Shakespeare is certainly implied. Furthermore, the opening lines quoted above are so closely aligned with Shylock's "Hath not a Jew eyes?" speech (3.1.53–66) as to provide an echo of what this kind of knowledge can enable, rhetorically and politically. That Brooks was playing in all-black productions of Shakespeare in Los Angeles two decades after he wrote these words is inspiring, but the fact that in *Merchant of Venice* he played not Shylock but the Prince of Morocco—a part infused with racial stereotypes—gives one pause. Did he bristle at the implications? Or did the adaptation problematize this role in ways that furthered the discussion of how Shakespeare could be spoken by and for the margins? The difficulty of answering such questions demonstrates the incomplete picture we have of what Shakespeare meant to racially and ethnically marginalized groups.

The most striking silence of all is the lack of Native American voices in Montana when it comes to the subject of the most famous European writer. As this book has demonstrated, the few places in which Native peoples figure into a Shakespearean story in Montana involve making fun of their ignorance or driving them off the land.[18] In neighboring North Dakota, a masque entitled *Shakespeare: The Playmaker* was performed in 1916 and included two Chippewas in the cast but no analogous performance records survive for Montana.[19] The Western Heritage Center of Billings, however, has a different kind of Shakespearean story to tell. One of the artifacts they hold is a medicine bag that belonged to a Northern Arapaho oral historian who was known as Bill Shakespeare. He chose this moniker when he began talking to anthropologists about his culture, for it symbolized "stature in the non-Indian world."[20] Without quoting the playwright or ever alluding to his works, Bill Shakespeare seemed to have understood "what's in a name."[21]

William Shakespeare the playwright was indeed white and middle class. But he also lived during a time of remarkable transition and an explosion of knowledge on all fronts. As Andrew Dickson notes, while Shakespeare's "physical existence was cramped and confined, [his] imagination roamed far and free." Shakespeare explored "worlds elsewhere" that were made possible by education, readily available books, and reports of travelers from distant lands.[22] The imaginative expansiveness that characterizes Shakespeare's works is founded upon a delight in alien places and peoples. Seen from this perspective, Shakespeare's popularity across the spectrum of Montana's citizens is natural, for this state is as polyglot and expansive as his imagination. Nonetheless, the colonial reality of this land has meant that some stories of Shakespearean encounters have been marginalized or silenced, while some were never even begun.

IN THE SCHOOLHOUSES

O, is it all forgot?
All school-days' friendship, childhood innocence?

—*A Midsummer Night's Dream*

In 1948, a London newspaper reported that "Shakespeare and the Montana cowboys are bringing English and American school girls closer together." This surprising statement was occasioned by a postwar exchange program that enabled a junior high teacher from Billings, Margaret Bettle, to spend a year instructing girls in a classroom in Finsbury Park, North London. During this time she developed pen pal connections between the girls in Montana and those in suburban London. The English schoolgirls "wanted to know more about the cowboys, buffalo, barbecues and other things in the great open spaces," whereas the girls in Billings received "letters reflecting the English girls' serious interest . . . in Shakespeare and other plays and poetry, and in English literature generally, which comprises most of their leisure reading."[1] Girls from these two allied nations on far removed continents expressed fascination based on cultural stereotypes: Shakespeare and cowboys. Yet such symbols, even when oversimplified, prove to be effective avenues for education.

Most people today first encounter Shakespeare precisely because he is part of the high school curriculum. Indeed, the Montana Common Core Standards for English language arts instruction list only one specific author as part of the requirements, and that author is Shakespeare.[2] The history of using Shake-speare as a pedagogical cornerstone in the West is as old as Montana's first one-room schoolhouses, such as Dimsdale's in Virginia City (see Figure 8). For many decades, most of Montana's students attended these small rural schools, where the multigrade format allowed for learning and mentoring across the age ranges. Ivan Doig, whose novel *The Whistling Season* concerns a rural com-munity and its one-room schoolhouse, notes that the "great overlooked fron-tier" in the first part of the twentieth century was Montana, because it was "the foremost homestead state, with a quarter of a million settlers taking up some thirty-two million acres." With this settling came the need for "heroic educa-tional efforts of those rural communities" that "stand forth as the lasting ben-eficial mark of the homesteading era."[3] Basic reading, writing, and arithmetic took place in these environments, but so did the study of Shakespeare. Whether in the country or the town schools, recourse to the stories and words of the most famous English writer was driven by a persistent belief that Shakespeare himself could speak across the centuries and across geography, serving as a ghostlike teacher.

Morality and Oratory

An actor, a rabbi, and a school superintendent walk into a high school audi-torium to talk about Shakespeare. This sounds like the opening of a great joke, but in fact this event, which took place in Butte in 1899, drew a large crowd that was interested in the topic—the lofty sounding "Shakespeare, the great apostle of Christianity." Frederick Warde was the actor at this event, and he noted that it was significant that "here on one platform are ranged represen-tatives of the school, the church and the stage, the three greatest factors in civilized mankind." Though obviously and intriguingly outside the dominant Christian discourse, the rabbi, Dr. Eisenberg, harped on a similar theme: "What the Bible is to religion," he wrote, "the work of Shakespeare is to cul-ture and mental development. He combines all the ingenuity, all the wisdom, all the culture, all the endowments of the immortals."[4] Warde and Eisenberg were two of many lecturers who toured across Montana, holding audiences spellbound with recitations from and discourses about the poems and plays.[5] Because these lectures invariably touched on the educational value of reading Shakespeare, sometimes the target audience was a younger population, who seemed to appreciate the attention. Warde's lecture to high school students in 1903 was greeted with applause and enthusiasm that "indicated the esteem in which he [was] held in the minds and hearts of the youth."[6] Such events foregrounded the importance of ceremony; at the end of Warde's lecture, the principal gave a commendatory speech and presented the actor with a shower bouquet of roses and made his own speech. The next year a lecturer named H. L. Southwick gave an address to students and teachers about Shakespeare and oratory, emphasizing the value of approaching the plays through performance. This insight, Southwick was convinced, would help teachers to understand how to reach their students so that the lessons they imparted would be heeded, for "the actor presents the unreal as though it were real, while the teachers and preachers present the real as though it were unreal."[7]

The teaching of Shakespeare in nineteenth-century America was guided by the McGuffey readers, which dominated curricular programs from 1836 to 1920. The readers did not present Shakespeare's plays in the context of characters' motivations and desires, but instead they excerpted speeches and took them out of context in order to study morality and rhetorical effectiveness.[8] William Holmes McGuffey was a devout Presbyterian, thus his objective was to enlist Shakespeare "in moral education and the formation of a citizenry."[9] The speeches used most often in the readers came from *Julius Caesar*, *Othello*, *King John*, *Henry VIII*, *Hamlet*, and *Merchant of Venice*. The influence of the readers is evident in the Fergus County curricular catalog from the early twentieth century, which outlines that the high schools in central Montana were progressing through *Merchant of Venice* in their first year, *Julius Caesar* in their second, and *Macbeth* in their third, with an emphasis on critical reading, understanding of style, character delineation through dialog, and rhetoric.[10]

Montana educators, however, built upon the McGuffey foundation to make sure that the students not only studied these speeches but performed them with proper decorum. Such skills were considered part of being a well-rounded, capable human being. In the first years of the twentieth century, Dillon was especially attuned to Shakespeare: not only was this the home of the active women's Shakespeare Club but also of the newly founded teachers college of Montana. On this fertile ground, those who taught Dillon's younger children developed ambitious programs, most notably an end-of-the-year Shakespearean entertainment performed annually by eighth graders. The students sang songs, acted out scenes, and gave speeches on topics such as "the greatness of the age of Elizabeth." During this period other more remote communities engaged in similar entertainments, showing the same interest in focusing school programs around Shakespeare. Students from the small town of Poplar on the Missouri River showcased a variety of skits, including *Merchant of Venice*'s scene between Portia and Nerissa, and Polonius's advice to Ophelia and Laertes in *Hamlet*. The latter was performed by a boy named William Walker, and the newspaper commended him for learning a long part, then made the connection between Shakespeare and morality clear with what sounds like an admonition: "We hope William may treasure these choicest bits of wisdom." The pageant concluded with a recitation of the oft-quoted Seven Ages of Man speech (*As You Like It*, 2.7.140–67), during which seven students entered one by one, each dressed to represent the age being described. Language and symbols were brought together to mark an occasion that commemorated what it means to pass from childhood to adulthood.[11]

The care with which such programs were put together is notable. Many performances were designed to accompany landmark events, such as graduations and the conclusion of the academic year. By excerpting these Shakespearean moments, students were able to practice their skills at oratory and music, to showcase poise and talent. The frequent occurrence of Shakespearean lectures throughout Montana assured that these students were well-versed not only in reading Shakespeare but in hearing the words declaimed and commented upon. The actors themselves were quick to reach out to the students, to serve as role models for wisdom and public speaking, such as Fritz Leiber, who gave a luncheon lecture on Shakespeare in Great Falls, where the featured guests were the high school basketball team and a group of sixth grade boys who sang songs.[12] Such an event testifies to an unexpected intersection between the status of a high school sports team, the musical talents of children, and the profound importance of Shakespeare's language. In a way, such a gathering worked to reflect, and to build, the ideal community.

As discussed in chapter 4, at the turn of the twentieth century Shakespeare was routinely viewed as a purveyor of moral insight. Educating with his words and works, showcasing the students' ability to entertain with these pieces, was a way of preserving the moral fabric of this frontier society. The benefits of such knowledge could become tangible, as when a young woman from Big Sandy gave a commendable lecture on the life and times of Shakespeare in 1920—an honor she received for having the highest marks in the class. Her reward for being the valedictorian was a four-year course at the state college, paving the way for her own training as a teacher.[13]

Little Eyases

In Act 2 of *Hamlet*, the Danish prince welcomes a troupe of players to Elsinore. When he inquires why they are traveling rather than in residence in the city, he is informed that they have been superseded by numerous theatrical companies comprised entirely of boys. Hamlet incredulously asks whether the "little eyases" (fledgling hawks) can possibly carry off these dramatic roles.[14] In this passage Shakespeare was commenting on a phenomenon close to home, for all-boy companies were indeed popular in London at the turn of the seventeenth century, posing an economic threat to Shakespeare's adult company. It's easy to see how Shakespeare (and Hamlet) have a point. After all, how good could child actors really be? And how could they ever portray serious adult issues and grapple with dense poetic language?

Teachers throughout the United States have long included Shakespeare in their curricula, in keeping with the approach laid out in the McGuffey readers. However, in Montana this phenomenon took an early and important turn: at every available opportunity, the "little eyases" across the fledgling state weren't just reading Shakespeare—they were performing him.[15] As early as 1892, there are accounts of high school students forming groups for the purpose of reading and studying Shakespeare but with a performative component.[16] With the dawn of the twentieth century, schools all over the state performed Shakespeare plays, usually in the local opera houses and replete with costumes ordered from big cities, full musical scores, and complete newspaper coverage.

The Great Falls newspapers proudly reported a 1919 production of *Comedy of Errors* and quoted the teacher/director as having very clear moral aims: "We are endeavoring to give an educational play, not something just for amusement," she said. The comedy, though entertaining, was chosen as an aid in educational development, with the amusement factor as only a secondary concern, for when it came to putting entertainment first, the teacher sternly remarked that "a sufficient variety of *that type* [of drama] may be seen down town."[17] Such a statement testifies to a moral agenda whereby the student performers were being educated by the Shakespeare curriculum, but they were in turn educating the adults who would otherwise stray to baser entertainments.

By far the most common play discussed and performed in Montana schools in the early twentieth century was *Merchant of Venice*. It is uncomfortable for us from a twenty-first-century perspective to imagine children staging this notorious play, full of anti-Semites (and perhaps anti-Semitic itself). Yet Montana educators in this period saw something very different in *Merchant of Venice*: a perfect vehicle for elocution and Christian morality, exemplified by Portia's famous set piece:

> The quality of mercy is not strained;
> It droppeth as the gentle rain from heaven
> Upon the place beneath. It is twice blest;
> It blesseth him that gives and him that takes:
> 'Tis mightiest in the mightiest; it becomes
> The throned monarch better than his crown ... (4.1.180–5)

This monologue combines poetry with logic and an important message about Christian charity, so it was an attractive text for educators. When Beaverhead County teachers gathered for a conference in 1903, one of the featured speakers explained the value of using *Merchant of Venice* in order to teach language; it was clearly the cornerstone of the Shakespeare curriculum in this period. The sheer number of schools engaging with this play is astounding, including those in the towns of Great Falls, Dillon, Big Timber, Plains, Roundup, Thompson Falls, and Plentywood—a list that testifies to Shakespeare's presence in every corner of the state.

Merchant of Venice's complexity allowed for students to revel in the comic antics of the clown Lancelot, the fairy-tale-inspired casket choices of Bassanio, or the elopement of Lorenzo and Jessica. But the play also invariably opened up areas for more serious discussion. One Big Timber reviewer of a 1907 high school production asserted in strikingly Marxist fashion that "the theme of the play is the relation of man to property." This article explained the problems in the play's society as a result of the merchant's loss of assets, which precipitated his need to enter into a borrowing economy with the Jew.[18] The popularity of *Merchant of Venice* onstage and off was of course largely centered upon the enigmatic character Shylock, whom some saw as full of evil intent, while others viewed him as warped by the violent and hypocritical behavior of the Venetian Christians. Recognizing a good debate topic when they saw one, the 1915 Roundup school wrestled with the question of whether "Shylock was more sinned against than sinning." The affirmative side won, but it is impossible to tell whether this was a result of beliefs or skilled debating.[19]

The Catholic Ursuline Academy in Great Falls staged costumed scenes from both *Winter's Tale* and *Merchant of Venice* in 1916 as part of their commencement exercises (see figure 24). The *Great Falls Tribune* noted that the statue scene from *Winter's Tale* would be especially welcome, for it promised "to be a very elaborate project and the big auditorium is admirably fitted for such a play."[20] Large, framed photos of this impressive production still hang on the walls at the Ursuline as a memorial to the students' full engagement with the complexity of Shakespeare's texts and their staging. In the early twentieth century the Ursulines also educated indigenous children at the nearby St. Peter's Mission in Cascade. This school, however, had a very different curriculum, designed to provide the Native children with "practical" skills. There is no evidence that these students were ever introduced to Shakespearean texts, so they never had a chance to ask questions about Shylock that would no doubt have seemed close to home.

For the Jewish community, however, there were some opportunities to engage with these issues. A Jewish lecturer named Leo Cooper spoke at Butte's Temple B'Nai in 1909 on the nature of Shylock. Cooper's view was that "consciously or not, Shakespeare protested against religious bigotry. He pictured Shylock as the result of the environment of the Hebrew and his hundreds of years of bitter brooding."[21] At the same time, Cooper assured, any educators who endeavored to teach this play had a responsibility to tell their pupils that Shylock was not a true representation of a Jew, because their people would never contemplate shedding blood or treating a daughter so callously.

The attempt to resolve the tension between the history of a people, Shakespeare as an artist, and the moral orientation of the twentieth century was likewise on the mind of a Plentywood High School girl. Her character sketch of Antonio, published in the local newspaper in 1919, concluded that "although he was kind to his Christian friends, Antonio had the fault of treating Jews too harshly for, as Shylock says, he spat on him, mocked him and called him a dog. Perhaps we cannot give Antonio the full blame for this because it

Figure 24. The "statue scene" in *The Winter's Tale* (5.3), performed by the students of the Ursuline Academy in Great Falls in 1916. The original photograph hangs on the wall at the Ursuline Academy. Photo by Kevin Brustuen, 2017.

was due to the times in which he lived."[22] Such a sensitivity extended to this student's view of Shakespeare: studying historical context enabled a consideration of how the playwright himself was susceptible to biases because of the times in which he lived.

While some saw in this play a fertile ground for moral debate and contemplation of other heavy topics, clearly the students enjoyed *Merchant of Venice*'s comic potential as well, as displayed in scenes featuring Portia and Nerissa, the suitors, and Launcelot Gobbo.[23] An even more popular trend was a burlesque called "*Merchant of Venice*: Up to Date."[24] The comedy sets the action in a high school, with Antonio as the captain of the Venetian football team and a gambler named Shylock betting on the opposing Belmont team and plotting to take a pound of hair from Antonio's football (rather than a pound of flesh from his body). This burlesque was originally written for a high school in Cedar Falls, Iowa, but the Montana schools loved it; between 1908 and 1920 it was produced in Billings, Cut Bank, Lewistown, Libby, Glasgow, Ekalaka, and Dillon.[25] These high school performances were often staged at the town opera houses to sold-out crowds, so they spared no labor in making these occasions successful, ordering professional costumes and devising musical accompaniment by children of all ages. One reviewer noted of "*Merchant of Venice:* Up to Date" that "the Jewish traits of [Shylock] are entirely omitted" in this version of the story. Removing the bigotry seems a natural choice for those interested in mining the comic potential of the play, just as it is for those interested in using it as a vehicle for moral instruction.

The idea of high school or elementary school students today performing *Merchant of Venice* is practically unheard of.[26] The history of Jewish oppression, especially in the wake of the Holocaust, makes approaches to the play notoriously difficult. Such challenging texts, however, can be useful teaching tools. Every year Shakespeare in the Schools, the fall educational outreach program of Montana Shakespeare in the Parks, brings eighty-minute performances of Shakespeare plays to high schools across the region. In 2015 the chosen play

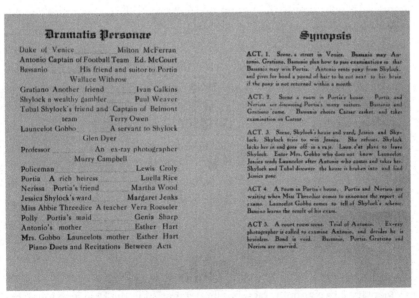

Figure 25. Program for "*The Merchant of Venice*: Up to Date," a popular burlesque that was performed by high schools throughout Montana. This program is from the Dillon High School performance in 1920. Photo by Kevin Brustuen, 2016.

was *Merchant of Venice*—not in spite of but because of the serious and difficult issues it raises. The production portrayed Shylock sympathetically, especially through its dark depiction of his forced conversion. Workshops with the students afterwards addressed bigotry and were designed to get students to see the nature of their own stereotypes and how they contribute to the culture of bullying. But the workshop model, like the lecture circuits from a century ago, depends on having professionally trained adults imparting knowledge to kids. Despite the value of such educational outreach, sometimes the greatest insights come from having the children take on the roles themselves.

Dreams and Tempests

The thrill of acting is intimately connected to the pleasures of childhood, for it offers a full entry into the land of make-believe, embracing magic and imagination. *A Midsummer Night's Dream* is an especially attractive play for children because of its setting in a fairy-inhabited forest. At a country school in Lake County in the Flathead Valley in the 1920s, the young students performed this comedy in a grassy meadow alongside a creek that "flowed gently along with wild flowers blooming on its banks." The children themselves supplemented the idyllic setting by making strings of crepe paper flowers, which they draped over the shrubs. Such a backdrop was ideal for this particular play but also created a complete immersion of the children into their natural landscape—something that made the potentially alien language of Shakespeare seem natural. Those who acted in this play spoke about it for years afterward, expressing nostalgia for the childhood pleasure of learning achieved through Shakespeare, poetry, and the natural world.[27]

Today the most popular play for young students is undoubtedly *A Midsummer Night's Dream*, attesting to an appetite for magic, impish fairies, and comedy of both the romantic and slapstick varieties.[28] Montana Shakes! (an outreach of MSIP) is the only touring Shakespeare program that is focused on elementary schools in the entire country. In 2017, three actor-educators ran intensive weeklong workshops for several schools that culminated in a mini-production of *A Midsummer Night's Dream*. One such site was Springhill Elementary, a two-room rural schoolhouse nestled in the Bridger Mountains just north of Bozeman. The kids, ranging from kindergarteners to eighth graders, wore fairy costumes and donkey heads, danced, and sang—all features

Figure 26. Children performing *A Midsummer Night's Dream* (directed by Stephanie Chavala and Miles Duffey) at the Springhill Elementary School on the edge of the Bridger Mountains. Next to the winged fairies are vocabulary words from the play that the children have been learning. Photo by Kevin Brustuen, 2017.

that could be true of any children's theatre production. But these young people also memorized and pronounced Shakespeare's words, while they recorded the new vocabulary on a large poster-board and paraphrased every line to make sure they knew what it meant. The directors emphasized the rhyming and the meaning of Shakespeare's original, showing how complex language can live in the body. As the director Stephanie Chavala put it, children of this age immediately grasp the unusual imagery with no impediment, and they embrace the seemingly alien language as if it were their own.[29]

Playing pretend is a natural part of childhood, and Shakespeare's works provide an imaginative arena that opens up multiple worlds. In the Springhill production one especially tiny girl proudly announced that, with her "lantern" and "thornbush," she was indeed the "*girl* in the moon."[30] Meanwhile, older students carried the story of the lovers forward, with Lysander played by a female. There was no concern about following gender norms in the love triangles. The resulting production achieved a fluidity between male and female, human and fairy, reality and imagination that is fitting for this play. A country school on the edges of an increasingly urban Bozeman served as the ideal staging ground where youth from different grades could work as an ensemble, across ages, genders, and expectations.[31]

Like *A Midsummer Night's Dream*, *The Tempest* is also about magic, but even more so about loss, forgiveness, and liberation. Two student performances of this play in 2017 show a great deal about what it means for young people to perform Shakespeare in Montana today.

Belt, Montana, has a population of five hundred. On Main Street a suspension bridge crosses the muddy creek, leading to an opera house that was erected a century ago and has been rechristened as the Belt Performing Arts Center. While the opera house was being renovated, there was a working rehearsal room with a thrust stage that was built by high school English and speech teacher Jeff Ross. Ross attended a Globe education seminar in London and became convinced that Belt students could fully realize Shakespeare through performance, so he created a troupe called the Belt Valley Shakespeare Players in 2013. Every year about a dozen students from a high school that has an enrollment of less than one hundred have participated in the productions. This organization has not grown in numbers, but it certainly has grown in reputation, as the students have performed not only in Belt but also in Great Falls, Missoula, Bozeman, and Helena.[32] Ross avers that "even with our material challenges, we have never identified ourselves as an 'underdog' because talent, energy, confidence, and perseverance are internal markers of individual and collective character."[33] Despite the competition for attention from Class C sports and a sometimes lackluster support from the community, the students show up at rehearsal, immerse themselves in these stories, and don costumes that allow them to be transported to a different world. Ross's understanding of how to engage with the rural experience of his students came to rest on the importance of geography—a word that is crucial in understanding a genre such as cowboy poetry, which "begins in the earth, the concrete (imagistically), and keeps a firm grasp on the physical, often the menial, the quotidian, a life that for many outsiders appears so Romantic."[34] In Belt, a community that was the home to Montana's first coal mine but now, like so many rural places in the state, struggles economically, the approach to Shakespeare that makes the most sense to the students is one that revels in the mysteries of an Elizabethan past while also being distinctively connected to a contemporary landscape.

A parallel organization in Bozeman called the Children's Shakespeare Society is made up of homeschool students from ages five to seventeen; they operate as an ensemble held together by a commitment to four-hundred-year-old plays. In 2017 they performed *The Tempest* to sold-out audiences. In this production a female Prospero presided over the action, accompanied by a trio of Ariels, while actors sang haunting songs, played violin, and staged an impressive shipwreck. The Children's Shakespeare Society's mission is to use Shakespeare as a vehicle for self-confidence and artistic expression—a marked difference from the educational objectives a century ago but at the same time an indicator of the ways in which Shakespeare can expand to suit the diverse ideologies of Montana across time.[35]

The Belt company that enacted *The Tempest* was almost entirely female—from the Ariel who jumped around the stage with sheer exuberance, to a crawling, athletic Caliban, to the commanding figure of Prospero. In the hands of the young female Prosperos in both productions, forgiveness was utterly achievable. The youth and promise of these performances suggested that grudges cannot be held indefinitely and that freedom is a real possibility. When Prospero abjured her magic and left Caliban on the island in the Bozeman production, Caliban turned to his former master and sang a song that was taken not from the play but from a mid-twentieth-century Italian resistance tradition. The song, called "Bella Ciao," speaks of the importance of freedom, which dovetails appropriately with Prospero's final line, "let your indulgence set me free." The entire company joined in this song at the end, singing an added verse written by directors Tonya Andrews and Gordon Carpenter:

Oh we are children and we are dreaming
Oh bella ciao, bella ciao, bella ciao, ciao, ciao
We are dreaming, for liberation
We want to change our world right now.

Four hours to the north, the Belt Valley Shakespeare Players also focused on the releasing of Caliban and Ariel. But while the spirit leaped happily to freedom, a much more unsettled feeling followed Caliban's release—the young woman playing this role elicited empathy, showing signs of trauma from years

Figure 27. Poster from the Belt Valley Shakespeare Players *Tempest* production (directed by Jeff Ross), which went to the Edinburgh Fringe Festival in 2017. Adrianna Irvine as Ariel, jumping in the Montana "ocean" of a wheat field. Photo by Elizabeth Harrison, 2017.

of captivity. She seemed unable to move, for she could neither become an integral part of Prospero's community nor return to precolonial life.

The Belt Valley Shakespeare Players received recognition from the American High School Theatre Festival and as a result were selected to perform their production of *The Tempest* at the fringe festival in Edinburgh, Scotland. Because they did not have enough actors from Belt to complete the cast, two members of the Children's Shakespeare Society of Bozeman joined them for the Edinburgh production, creating a strong link between the different demographics but similar missions of these companies. The promotional picture for this production showed Ariel jumping in a Montana field of wheat. Many of these actors had not even seen the ocean, much less traveled abroad, and yet Shakespeare enabled a world in which everything seemed uncannily possible.[36]

Such Shakespearean stories about freedom can certainly be inspiring. However, *The Tempest* is frequently used to talk about colonial conquest and subjugation of native peoples. How does the play speak, if at all, to Montana's indigenous population? Johanna Moore, a high school teacher in Colstrip, which is on the edge of both the Northern Cheyenne and the Crow Indian Reservations, taught *The Tempest* and found that her students immediately connected their situations to those of Prospero's servants. They thought of Caliban as Northern Cheyenne, for, as one student remarked, "it was just like the white man to make them look bad because they wouldn't do what they were told. [The student] said that they did the same to Chief Dull Knife when he led his people back to Montana," and "the Northern Cheyenne were punished for years for rebelling against the government." Another student who is part Crow noticed that "Ariel was smart like the Crow. Play along with the white man and get what you can because it is their world."[37] These students saw in Shakespeare's characters a parallel to their own histories—a stark reality in which the receipt of land and money is dependent upon cooperation with a colonizing force.

Shakespeare himself doubted whether children could perform difficult drama, but Montana education has embraced the idea for over a century, with diverse and compelling results. The "brave new world" of the *Tempest* (5.1.183) speaks to a regional identity that is associated with sheer size, variety, independence, and possibility. Shakespeare, even when taken up by "little eyases," is big enough, expansive enough, for the stages of our imaginative and geographical landscapes.

Shakespeare in College

Montana's earliest high schools and elementary schools staged more Shakespearean plays and entertainments than its colleges. Nonetheless, by the end of the nineteenth century English and drama departments were formed at universities throughout America, and with this development Shakespeare's works became a staple of postsecondary education. At Montana's state university in Missoula, students themselves dove into literary activities, forming several book and drama clubs. One group called on Daniel Bandmann to help with the founding of a dramatic club, and as a result the Quill and Dagger Society (later the Masquer Theatre Organization) gained a vibrant life. The club read and performed plays, including those by Shakespeare, throughout much of the twentieth century, even occasionally traveling around the state to do so.

Universities in Montana recruited heavily for faculty members, most of whom had received degrees from universities in the Midwest or on the East Coast, and with such a westward influx came more opinions about the import of Shakespeare. In 1901 Lucy Carson, having just graduated from the University of Chicago with an English degree, took a job at the normal college in Dillon, where she installed Shakespeare as a regular part of the curriculum. For four decades she influenced teachers across the state, ensuring that Montana's young people received an education that included the English Renaissance. Carson led both the women's Shakespeare Club and the university drama department, instilling a deep devotion to education through performance. One tribute to Carson noted that "her college students and the Dillon Shakespeare club of which she was the leader were given the inspiration of guidance by a scholar whose appreciation of history and human motives was cosmopolitan in scope."[38] Her knowledge was enhanced when she took courses at Columbia University during a sabbatical, but she returned to Dillon to share what she had learned, also writing articles for the *Normal College Index* about topics such as the stage and critical interpretations of Shylock that concluded with a bibliography designed for the teacher of Shakespeare.[39] One year, rather than directing a classical play, she decided to direct a comedy called *Dear Brutus* that was written by Sir James Barrie (of *Peter Pan* fame). At the convocation in Dillon Carson discussed Barrie's *Dear Brutus* and its echoes of both *Julius Caesar* and *A Midsummer Night's Dream*. In this speech, one audience member reflected, Carson "told so much truth whimsically, understandingly, and yet hopefully for those of 'thin bright faces.'"[40] In addition to influencing scores of students, Carson donated her impressive collection of books, some to the university and others to the town of Dillon; to this day the public library has a turret that is designated as the Lucy Carson alcove, which was originally envisioned as a repository for the plays that she loved so much. University of Montana Western also has a library named for Lucy Carson. An ex libris bookplate used in this library's collection identifies books that belonged to her, and the decorative image on this label serves as further testimony to Carson's association with Shakespeare. The cover shows a drawing of *The Tempest*, and in the upper right-hand corner is the famous quotation "We are such stuff as dreams are made on" (4.1.56–57). The picture itself shows the ideal combination between Shakespeare's imagined landscape (a stormy sea, a craggy island) and a decidedly Montana touch: the island is dotted with evergreen trees.

We might expect a vibrant interest in Shakespeare at a teachers college such as the one where Carson was a faculty member, but students in very different kinds of programs also gravitated to the idea of performing his plays. For instance, the agricultural college in Bozeman sponsored a well-attended lecture by Frederick Warde, who spoke on Shakespeare's interpretation of oratory.[41] Not content merely to hear about Shakespeare, the students at the Butte School of Mines performed *Twelfth Night* in the engineering building in 1931, with sixteenth-century period costumes ordered from Los Angeles, artistic lighting effects, and music.[42] Such activities among the students at the School of Mines was a continuation of Butte's booming theatrical culture at the turn of the twentieth century; Shakespeare was still a staple part of culture and learning, regardless of the career path.

The state colleges in Missoula, Dillon, and Bozeman increasingly took interest in Shakespeare on stages as well as in the classrooms, but some of the most vibrant Shakespearean culture was at Helena's small liberal arts institution, Carroll College.[43] The student newspaper, *The Prospector*, is full of allusions to, reports about, and articles concerning Shakespeare. No doubt the funniest of these comes from a student in 1923 who decided to provide an updated, thoroughly Montana-based summary of *King Lear*. This detailed parody of the play imagines "Mr. King Lear" as a lumber baron and Gloucester as a washed-up gambler. Clever notes about the settings include "Reagan's hunting lodge," "Gloucester's den of iniquity," "Duke of Albany's poultry farm," and "alfalfa fields near Dover." The adaptation is impressively detailed, imagining each scene in a setting and with a plot appropriate to this Montana version of the story. The angle on Kent is perhaps the most creative, including details about his disguise ("Kent comes in with his face washed. The disguise completely fools Lear. He tells him he's a vegetarian and wants to work for him."). When Kent encounters the servant Oswald in Shakespeare's play, Kent voices a series of insults that give full range to the linguistic possibilities of English in 1605 (the year *King Lear* was written). The Carroll College spoof is nearly as impressive as Shakespeare's original, for this Kent launches into "You white-livered, garlic-eating boloney; tryin' to act like a gent when you're only a one horse piano hustler. You can't go in the park cause the squirrels will eat you. You're a case of weather proof brains on a double distilled hick and your teeth ain't the only ivory in your bean." The colorful language captures not only the moment of the student rewriting of the play but also its original flavor. The final line of the work articulates an impressively accurate way to look at the ending of *King Lear*: "Kent is busted and disgusted, so Albany and Edgar have to run the state and fite over the will." This is followed, in mock-Renaissance style, by "Exeunt, out of step." The anonymous article printed in the Carroll College newspaper claims, tongue in check, that this summary was written "owing to the study that is being made of this classic, in the institutions of learning thruout the U.S."[44] For all the parody involved, though, it is abundantly clear that the author(s) knew Shakespeare's play intimately and thought in creative ways about what it would mean to translate it to a contemporary setting. Such innovation shows that Shakespearean mythology could be overlaid with Western mythology in 1920s Montana.

Undoubtedly the golden age of university Shakespeare performances was the 1950s and 1960s. These decades saw the growth of theatre programs, and in Montana this was reflected by a burgeoning interest in performing Shakespeare, as well as works by his contemporaries, at state colleges as well as at Carroll College.[45] Alongside the successful production of many Shakespearean plays, however, there was a growing sense that these works were difficult to produce and to convey to a contemporary audience. When the Montana Masquers of Missoula visited Carroll College with their *Othello* production in 1955, the director said that "Shakespeare's plays are exceptionally difficult to stage, especially in Montana because of the difference in the culture of Western theatre goers to that of the Broadway stage."[46] This comment registers a perceived gap between Montana and Shakespeare that did not occur to the mountain men and yet seemed (at least to some) to be nearly insurmountable in the later half of the twentieth century. This difficulty had also been articulated by a reviewer who did not like the same company's 1951 production of *Macbeth* because "some 300 years after the poet's death, in Missoula, Montana, Shakespeare seems to have lost a good deal of his power. The Montana Masquers staged his 'Macbeth' as if it were a drama out of a middle-class living room."[47] The desire to make Shakespeare relevant to their own societies caused students to explore ways to speak to modern settings and contexts, but sometimes this left the audiences hungry for the grander, more sweeping poetic quality that so many associate with Shakespeare.

When the College of Great Falls mounted a production of *Hamlet* in 1962, the artistic team was seeking this kind of grandeur, hoping to return to a drama that would be "actable" because "its characters don't just sit around as in most contemporary plays."[48] The abstract design and special stage built for the performance heightened the quest for symbolic meaning. The production showed, too, the ways in which theatre could work as a community endeavor. A reviewer noted that this *Hamlet* was "Staged in the college theater, directed by a college instructor," and blended "on-and off-stage talents of college students and faculty with the talents of and skills of students and adults from the city of Great Falls and from Malmstrom Air Force Base."[49] One of the primary functions of universities is to provide crucial connections between education and the wider community. Theatre is an effective vehicle for such endeavors, and during the turbulent decade of the 1960s the time was ripe for figuring out how Shakespeare could become part of this mission.

In southwest Montana's theatre history, no one was more influential than Ben Tone, who was a cofounder of the Virginia City Players, a director at the Loft Theatre in Bozeman, a faculty member in the theatre department of MSU, and a mentor to countless theatre artists. His directorial work at MSU from 1960 to 1982 was multifaceted, covering playwrights as varied as Sophocles, Dickens, Brecht, O'Neill, and Beckett. Tone directed *Macbeth* in 1970, but at MSU his most remembered Shakespearean moment was when he took on the role of King Lear in a 1978 production. Despite MSU's origin as a university focused on agriculture and engineering, the theatre department had become robust in the 1960s and 1970s under the leadership of Tone, Joe Fitch, and Bruce Jacobsen. A review of the *King Lear* production by English professor Michael Sexson thus commended the high production values of this endeavor, for there were "sumptuous costumes, impressively choreographed fight sequences and well-crafted scenery" that "helped to make this version of 'Lear' a visual feast." But the real star of the play, in every way, was Tone, who managed to convey the sublime nature of the tragedy. In Sexson's estimation, Tone brought out the "contradictory elements of man's nature—the fallen and the transcendent."[50] In the late 1970s, after the last troops had been brought home from Vietnam, the horrors of King Lear's repeated cries of "Never" in the final scene were agonizing. The twentieth century had begun with schoolchildren reciting speeches about Christian mercy from *Merchant of Venice*, but Shakespeare was employed toward the century's end to teach a different lesson: how to cope with our own catastrophic failures.

INTERLUDE 5
ARTISTS

Exit, pursued by a bear.
—*The Winter's Tale*

Montana artists—whether novelists, poets, painters, or photographers—are frequently haunted by the grandeur of the landscape but equally by the smallest elements of nature that constitute the majesty of larger visions. These artists have often found companionship in Shakespeare, drawn to his immense significance, but even more often to the particular qualities of his words.

A prolific photographer of the early twentieth century, Evelyn Cameron, was born in Britain to a wealthy merchant-class family, but she embraced a very different life, moving with her husband to eastern Montana and managing a ranch near the town of Terry. Cameron's photographs cover an array of landscapes, animals, and people, and she also kept a journal detailing her activities. In 1913 Cameron spent some time visiting a friend's home in the Highwood Mountains; during that time she erected a blind so that she could approach birds unobserved. One day she took her cameras to that spot and awaited the swans and the lighting for an ideal photo. She wrote in her diary that to pass the time during the excursion she read the entirety of *Merchant of Venice*. This casual record of her activity on one February day is one of many examples that show Cameron's regular reading of Shakespeare (her diary

Figure 28. Two swans in a photo taken by Evelyn Cameron on April 8, 1913. In her diary Cameron records that she read *The Merchant of Venice* while waiting for the right conditions to capture a photo of swans. Evelyn J. Cameron Photograph Collection, PAC-87.G081-014. Montana Historical Research Center archives.

records that she also read *Hamlet* that year), but this particular experience is especially appropriate, for the connection between Montana's swans and the swan of Avon was clearly on her mind.

Cameron's photographs are some of the first ever taken of birds in their natural habitat in the West. She is even more well-known, however, for the way that she captured the realities of frontier life—the everyday activities of the women and men, set against the background of the eastern Montana landscape. These photos are striking in part because of Cameron's taste for the theatrical; as biographer Kristi Hager describes it, "Photo shoots became quite the spectacle; people stopped what they were doing to participate in the production. Cameron was the director. The camera's large viewing screen was like a stage on which she composed tableaus."[1] Cameron's taste for the dramatic in her photographs was fueled by her love for Shakespeare, but in her private thoughts about what it meant to interact with people, she also turned to his words, using a quotation from *Much Ado about Nothing* to lament that "friendship is constant in all other things save in the office and affairs of love."[2] The interpersonal catalyst for this entry is lost to us, but whatever the situation, Cameron found Shakespeare an insightful companion, whether she wanted to consider nature or humanity. The physical presence of a Shakespearean book in Cameron's eastern Montana landscapes is a recurring motif, recalling the "tongues in trees" of *As You Like It* but also the drowning of Prospero's books in *The Tempest* (5.1.57).

The desire to capture the natural environment has become a defining feature of Montana's visual arts, from the elaborate paintings and murals of Charlie Russell to the ranching photographs of Evelyn Cameron. The same investment in the landscape infuses the work of writers, as can be seen from memoirs about growing up in rural Montana such as Ivan Doig's *This House of Sky* and Mary Clearman Blew's *All but the Waltz*. Doig's array of novels has placed him as one of the most widely recognized Montana authors, largely because of his memorable writing about the elusive place called the West. But for Doig, language came before place. He wrote: "I don't think of myself as a 'western' writer. To me language—the substance on the page, that poetry under the prose—is the ultimate 'region,' the true home for a writer."[3] In this respect Doig is similar to Norman Maclean, whose novella *A River Runs through It*, which was made into the popular 1992 film, fostered a fascination and romanticizing of fly-fishing in western Montana's magnificent rivers.

Maclean's upbringing was accompanied by strict attention to the rhythms of life—in nature, in theology, and in poetry. Fly-fishing casts were taught with a metronome, theology with a catechism, and poetry with scansion. In this last department, it was Norman's mother who played the most important part. In his short story "USFS 1919," Maclean recalls that his high school teacher had wanted them to write sonnets, but he wasn't able to do it. He begged his mother for help, and she sat with him at the table "with Milton or Shakespeare between us, and . . . I held her left hand and with her right hand she would beat out the accented syllables. Then we would write lines of our own iambic pentameter, and our blank verse, unlike Milton's or Shakespeare's, never had any little odds or ends left over."[4] Maclean narrates this touching story of learning how to scan poetry with his mother against a decidedly more sordid background. He thinks of iambic meter because he has awoken in a brothel with alarmingly thin walls and hears the people next door screaming at one another. He is struck by the rhythms of the woman's language, how "You lousy bastard" and "You are as crooked as a tub of guts" are iambic, natural like Shakespeare's language, rather than forced as his own attempts at writing poetry had been.[5]

At the end of this story, Maclean laments because this was the last time he crossed the Bitterroot, and everything passed away, except, perhaps, the words and some poetry. Maclean's own attention to poetry in his writing is not surprising, for he spent more than thirty years teaching Shakespeare and the Romantic poets at the University of Chicago. It was here that former Supreme Court justice Paul Stevens took Maclean's courses. Stevens later remarked that "the best way to prepare for law is to take Shakespeare from Norman Maclean."[6]

Maclean's approach was decidedly technical; he spent an entire class period discussing the opening line of *Hamlet*: "Who's there?" Maclean found that the "greatness" of Shakespeare was inseparable from the writing itself. "Every year I said to myself, 'You better teach this bastard so you don't forget what great writing is like.'"[7] Such a particularized approach is evident in the article that Maclean wrote about Shakespeare: "Episode, Scene, Speech, and Word: The Madness of Lear" (1952). As the title indicates, Maclean was interested in progressing from the general to the specific, thus although he saw Lear's thoughts as being of universal significance, he was most interested in how such revelations include all of us, in the most singular way. The last part of his article analyzes Lear's line "Hast thou given all to thy two daughters, and art thou come to this?" (3.4.48–49). In the economy of this line, Maclean sees the enormity of Lear's tragedy, the supreme expression of fear and pity: "Our task, therefore, is to look again at these few, short, ordinary words to see how they add up to what our feelings tell us is something very big."[8] Proceeding through diction and grammar, Maclean eventually reads the essence of tragedy, its fear and pity, within the rhythms of Shakespearean language itself. Whether Maclean was looking at fly-fishing, smoke jumping, or literature, it was the craft that interested him most.[9] How appropriate it is that the writer who has come to epitomize Montana as the "Last Best Place" saw the language of Shakespeare as the most striking place of all.

When it comes to the American West, sometimes it is difficult to know where the poetry ends and nature begins. This was something that the naturalist and father of the conservation movement in the West, John Muir, also

Figure 29. Norman Maclean teaching his Shakespeare class at the University of Chicago. Photo by Leslie Strauss Travis, 1970.

understood quite well. During his boyhood in Scotland, Muir was raised on the Bible, Robert Burns, and Shakespeare, and the words of these writers reinforced his nature writings. As he hiked through Yosemite, then toured the Pacific Northwest and Yellowstone, Muir kept journals in which his poetic reflections attempted to capture the majesty of nature. Like Cameron, he loved to read while doing his work outside, thus he wrote of "luxuriating in Shakespeare" while tending sheep. He was attuned to some of Shakespeare's favorite metaphors, such as the "book of nature" (*Antony and Cleopatra*, 1.2.10), "the music of the spheres" (*Pericles*, 5.1.217), and "this earth of majesty, this seat of Mars" (*Richard II*, 2.1.41). Perhaps his favorite Shakespearean quotation, though, was from *Troilus and Cressida*—"One touch of nature makes the whole world kin" (3.3.176)—for the ecological interdependency of natural and human environments is the foundation of Muir's writings and beliefs. Musing about an encounter he had with the animal world in the High Sierra, he wrote that he was eager to meet all of the mountain animals, many of whom introduced themselves willingly, "though in my first interview with a Sierra bear we were frightened and embarrassed, both of us, but the bear's behavior was better than mine."[10] Of another meeting with a bear, Muir wrote: "I was afraid to run, lest he should be encouraged to pursue me; therefore I held my ground, staring him in the face within a dozen yards or so, putting on as bold a look as I could."[11] With his love of Shakespeare as well as nature, it is difficult not to see in the background of such a statement an awareness of *The Winter's Tale*'s famous stage direction: "*Exit, pursued by a bear*" (3.3.57).

Half a century later and much closer to Montana, the British poet laureate Ted Hughes also thought of Shakespeare when he encountered a bear. Hughes's poem "The 59th Bear" describes an experience in Yellowstone National Park when he and Sylvia Plath traveled there in 1959. He writes that a bear broke into their car, "and on claw hooks lifted out our larder. / He'd left matted hairs. I glued them in my Shakespeare." Throughout the poem Hughes equates the wilderness with a dark malign force, ultimately prophesying Plath's death:

> At that time
> I had not understood
> How the death hurtling to and fro
> Inside your head, had to alight somewhere
> And again somewhere, and had to be kept moving,
> And had to be rested
> Temporarily somewhere.[12]

Hughes makes sense of his experience by returning to the words and the book in an attempt to contain the unbridled dark energies of the wild. It is this urge that propels Hughes to glue the remnants of the bear's violent destruction into his Shakespeare book. Whether photographers, painters, or writers, many artists in the Northern Rockies have given expression to the delicate interplay between nature and civilization by bringing Shakespeare along with them. The resulting artistic expressions are invariably like Hughes's palimpsest—a Shakespeare changed by the texture of the West.

FREEING SHAKESPEARE

As you from crimes would pardoned be,
Let your indulgence set me free.

—*The Tempest*

It is June 2018. At MSU's duck pond, one thousand audience members gather to watch Montana Shakespeare in the Parks' production of *Othello*, performed on a two-level stage with a staircase and enhanced by electric lights and a sound system. The ten-actor cast consists of professionally trained actors from all over the United States; none of them are from Montana. The costumes and set evoke the Napoleonic era, and a supporting crew of thirty people (designers, costumers, etc.) has been hired to put the show together. The actors will go on to perform seventy-six times in sixty-one towns, not just in Montana but also on the edges of four surrounding states.

It is June 1973. At MSU's Hannon Hall, one hundred audience members gather to watch MSIP's performance of scenes from four Shakespearean comedies. The sixteen actors are students, professors, and community members who perform on a simple set in Elizabethan costumes with no amplification or special effects. They'll go on to perform this show thirteen times in seven communities that are all short drives from Bozeman.

The differences between these scenes point to the growth and development

139

of Montana's most beloved cultural organization. In the history of MSIP, much has changed with the times, but the more remarkable fact is that the essential mission of this company has been consistent: to provide high-quality productions of Shakespeare's plays to the people of Montana, especially to small communities, free of charge. The mission, growth, and success of the company have resulted in the most remarkable identification of the state with Shakespeare. The *State by State* book mentioned in the preface emblazons Montana with Shakespeare's face because of the powerful legacy of MSIP. However, as *Shakespeare in Montana* has shown, MSIP is not the origin but instead the culmination of a long history of encounters with Shakespeare that have become inextricably woven together with the identity of the state.

Origins

Bruce Jacobsen was a Montana native who took up a position as a professor in the Media Theatre Arts Department at MSU in the late 1960s. MSIP was his creation, and when it launched in 1973 it was sponsored by MSU's Summer School Cultural and Recreational Program. Jacobsen's passion to provide free outdoor theatre in an informal setting was fueled by a desire to show audience members that Shakespeare can be fun, thus his productions emphasized the light, comic side of the plays. The 1973 season featured scenes performed by amateurs, but in the second year Jacobsen had already made changes that have stayed with the company ever since: performing two plays in repertory, with professionally trained actors. Jacobsen tapped into the troubadour tradition in those early seasons, incorporating acrobatics, juggling, and music as part of the performances. The simplicity of the Elizabethan costumes and setting (designed by Jacobsen's colleague Signe Anderson) also lent themselves to a pared down, flexible staging that was easily mobile. With this sort of troupe Jacobsen could achieve his dream "to take theatre to the people rather than bring people to the theatre."[1]

By 1976 another tradition arose: often the season featured not two Shakespearean plays but one by Shakespeare and another classic comedy by a playwright such as George Bernard Shaw or Molière. Audience members around Montana reacted to the traveling troupe with enthusiasm. Newspapers featured articles in praise of the shows, printing pictures of the actors as well as audience members of all ages who came to take in the only live theatrical

Figure 30. The inaugural season of MSIP (1973), directed by Bruce Jacobsen. Photo courtesy of MSIP archives.

event that many of the towns had ever hosted. What has always seemed important about MSIP's success is the wide cross-section of audience members it reaches—people from all walks of life in a state that has its own subtle diversities. Jacobsen averred that "the town size doesn't matter," so the actors have always traveled both to larger communities such as Billings and Great Falls and to towns with populations under two thousand, such as Baker and Plains. The cumulative effect, however, has been the ability to reach a total audience of more than 900,000 over the past forty-seven years.

The ubiquitous young people who attend MSIP performances have been a special part of MSIP's mission.[2] Children routinely run up to the actors after a show, begging for their autographs, or ask whether they can help to take the set down at the end of the evening. Sometimes the MSIP performance is the central entertainment for a twelve-year-old's birthday party, or kids pile onto a railroad car at a historical museum to get a better view of the stage. These young people often understand what it means to be invested in keeping MSIP's mission going; in 1977 a ten-year-old girl from Utica wrote to the MSIP office, praising the show and enclosing her own one-dollar donation.[3] The children's desire to contribute to the company in whatever way they can has remained as strong as ever since that time.

In 1980 Jacobsen left MSU to take a job in North Dakota, and Joel Jahnke, who had been the scenic designer and an MSU professor since 1977, took over as artistic director. Under Jahnke's leadership, the company grew and the programs expanded, especially driven by increased funding from sources such as the National Endowment for the Arts and corporate sponsors such as Subaru. By the time Jahnke retired in 2013, the summer season had expanded to sixty communities, there were fall and spring school tours, fund-raising events, and multiple staff members who were vital to coordinate the many aspects of the company.[4]

MSIP's reputation has extended far beyond Montana, for the company has been featured in news outlets such as the *New York Times*, the *Wall Street Journal*, *NBC Nightly News*, and *PBS* (both in the feature documentary *Bard in the Backcountry* and in *Shakespeare Uncovered*). Such recognition has continued under the leadership of Jahnke's successor, Kevin Asselin, who was an actor, company manager, and fight choreographer for several years before becoming the executive artistic director in 2014. Asselin has continued to follow MSIP's core mission, while also expanding the quality and outreach

Figure 31. MSIP's *Macbeth* production (directed by Kevin Asselin), performed in Eureka in 2017. Children watch the play from a historic train car. Photo by Kevin Brustuen.

of its educational programs and adding an annual professional winter production of a non-Shakespearean play in MSU's Black Box Theatre.[5]

The Wild West

When MSIP launched its elementary school tour in 2008, the show was entitled "All the West's a Stage." The framework featured three characters of the "Old West" (Augustus Babylon, Johnny Dropbottom, and Mary Sweetgrace) who were traveling around Montana performing Shakespeare. Such a concept highlights an important facet of the region's history: "The West" has always been a performance. Buffalo Bill understood as much when he developed his Wild West roadshow, which ran from 1881 to 1917, performing "cowboys and Indians" for spectators who wanted to witness iconic western figures and attendant fantasies of lawlessness, even as they sensed their own shrinking frontiers. At first glance, transposing an Englishman from a remote past onto a Wild West imagined landscape seems somewhat disjunctive. However, Buffalo Bill himself loved to envision what it would look like if he were to perform Shakespeare's plays. Responding to critics who complained that his "low-brow" entertainments were driving out Shakespearean actors such as Edwin Booth, Buffalo Bill bragged that he would "do *Hamlet* in a buckskin suit, and when my father's ghost appears 'doomed for a certain time,' &c., I shall say to Jack, 'Rope the cuss in Jack!' . . . As 'Richard the Third,' I shall fight with pistols and hunting knives. In 'Romeo and Juliet' I shall put a half-breed squaw on the balcony and make various other interpretations of Shakespeare's words to suit myself."[6] Buffalo Bill was a master of blurring the lines between fantasy and reality, of using the icons of the West in a self-referential manner, so it is not surprising that he saw ways in which the endlessly adaptable Shakespeare could be entirely at home in the American West. This tradition is part of what has enabled the success of MSIP and has also made the Old West settings delightful for audiences.

In MSIP's history, no play has been performed more often than *The Taming of the Shrew*.[7] In both 1989 and 2015, the play was set in the nineteenth-century West. The 1989 production was directed by MSIP veteran actor/director Tom Morris and included favorite western songs such as "Don't Fence Me In." The year was appropriate for the production because it was the centennial of Montana's statehood. Morris envisioned the play as a sort of fantasy placed in a Montana ghost town that mysteriously disappeared in 1889 and was reappearing throughout the summer of 1989.[8] Because Shakespeare wrote a frame for *Taming of the Shrew* that shows a drunkard named Christopher Sly watching the play, there is ample opportunity to suggest multiple time periods. In 1989, Sly was envisioned as "Wild" Bill Shakespeare—an overlay of Wild Bill Hickok as symbol of the lawless West and Shakespeare as the author of the fantasy. The costumes lent a great deal of flavor to the play and caused one newspaper headline to dub this "Shakespeare in Chaps." This article further explains the creative combination between the nineteenth century and the 1980s that the production design evoked: "In lieu of the English bard's soliloquies, the cast, with tongue-in-cheek humor, substituted cowboy ballads. As a spoof on cowboy chaps, various members of the cast showed up in a reasonable facsimile of white angora, tiger skin and leopard printed leg coverings."[9]

Asselin's 2015 production had a more unified period design that located the play in the nineteenth century, but these costumes were not merely for show: he also wanted to use them to emphasize disparity between socioeconomic classes. Claudia Boddy's costume designs supported this concept by showing a "contrast between clean, well-polished edges for the wealthy characters versus distressed canvas or leather on the gun slinger, hard-working ranch and farm hands."[10] For Asselin the western setting was a way to make the show seem relevant to members of the Montana communities, but it also proved to be "a great deal of fun to find new ways of keeping Shakespeare's stories alive."[11]

Both productions used the western theme to bring out the play's physical humor; scenes featured characters with lariats and guns who were prone to fistfights that could get them thrown out of the local saloon. The violence of the society (Montana in Morris's production and South Pass City, Wyoming, in Asselin's) extended to the courtship in Shakespeare's play. In this setting, Petruchio's "taming" of Kate included physical gestures that mimicked riding bucking broncos and roping calves. Such interactions, however, highlighted the uncomfortable gender politics of this play. Morris handled this difficult dimension of *Taming of the Shrew* by making the misogyny a fantasy that was part of an imagined West: "The Elizabethan thing tends to get a little misogynistic," Morris admitted, "but if you set [Petruchio] up as a gunfighter, it's part of the Wild West cliché and a little more believable." Jahnke agreed that this approach "puts the chauvinistic portion of the play in perspective—it makes it a sort of fantasy."[12] Another way that the productions pushed back against gender stereotypes was by featuring rugged female gunfighters—Morris cast Kate as an Annie Oakley figure, and Asselin changed Petruchio's servant Grumio into Grumia, who resembled Calamity Jane. In the latter adaptation, Grumia was a rough product of Wyoming's lawless society, but as a woman she also looked with disapproval at the way Kate was being treated. Making Grumio into a female character from nineteenth-century Wyoming deliberately reflected upon the history of the women's suffrage movement, especially this state's proud place as the first to give women the right to vote.

The West in both productions was depicted as lawless but also diverse (Morris found ways to evoke a checkerboard of Montana that included bandidos, cowhands, prospectors, and Chinese immigrants). At the same time, Morris's setting echoed Shakespeare's depiction of Padua as a hypocritical society that labeled vocal women as shrews and privileged the superficial and

Figure 32. MSIP's 2015 *Taming of the Shrew* production (directed by Kevin Asselin), which was set in the nineteenth-century American West. Erika Haaland as Katherine, Torsten Johnson as Petruchio, and Sarah Dunnavant as Grumia. Photo courtesy of Winslow Studio and Gallery.

spoiled Bianca. Both Morris and Asselin found in Petruchio and Kate's relationship a truer, more genuine understanding that allowed them to rise above the problems inherent in the relationships around them. The surprise twist at the end of the 2015 production was that when Petruchio asked Kate to explain to the women "what duty they do owe their lords and husbands," he pointed not to Bianca or the Widow when he said, "and first begin with her,"[13] but to Hortensio. In this way, the entire speech that Kate gave about womanly obedience was turned on its head; as befits the lawless West, gender dynamics and power were anything but settled by the end of the play.

The Wild West setting has not been limited to MSIP's productions of *Taming of the Shrew*, for it also served as a compelling backdrop for the 2013 Shakespeare in the Schools production of *Two Gentlemen of Verona* (also directed by Asselin). In that adaptation, Valentine's departure at the beginning of the play was not just to another city, but he was in fact leaving rural Montana and going to Boston. Even in the midst of the eastern city, however, he found solace in an aptly named Sylvia; his habitation in the woods outside Boston was a return to nature that allowed him to rescue Sylvia when Proteus attempted to rape her. Just as in *The Taming of the Shrew*, this production's western setting allowed for connections to Montana's past but also for reflections upon histories of violence against women, both in Shakespeare's play and on the Montana frontier. In an article about the 1989 *Taming of the Shrew*, Sharon Beehler and Sara Jayne Steen noted, "In a sense, Kate is like the Western landscape itself."[14] The parallels between taming the feminine and taming the landscape evoke the fantasies of male conquest that have been so powerful, and destructive, in the West. MSIP's western-themed productions have thus shown that Shakespeare's unsettling storylines find new relevance when they are transferred to both present and past Montana eras.

Buffalo Bill died around the time that motion pictures were bringing into being a genre called the western. He would well have appreciated the power of film in creating the myth of The West. Later in the twentieth century, another Bill—actor Bill Pullman—grew up watching westerns, so he was excited to see the places that the filmic imagination had imparted to him.[15] Pullman agreed to be part of MSIP in 1978 not because he wanted to "do Shakespeare" but because he wanted to be out West. And the sense that Montana is home has never left him. After an enormously successful acting career that included Broadway credits as well as films such as *Ruthless People*, *Sleepless in Seattle*, *While You Were Sleeping*, and *Independence Day*, Pullman starred in a 2017 western called *The Ballad of Lefty Brown*, which was filmed in five Montana locations.[16] Pullman also managed to return to his MSIP history by populating some of the scenes with extras, including Joel Jahnke, Tom Morris, and John Hosking. Like the self-referential productions of *The Taming of the Shrew* set in the Wild West, this nod to the veteran actors and directors of MSIP was an insider reference to the past that these men shared: all Montana roads lead to Shakespeare.

The Land

Performing Shakespeare outdoors is a popular endeavor, especially in North America. It offers a sense of returning to the Elizabethan past (since the original Shakespearean theatres were also open air) but more importantly provides a family-oriented, summertime atmosphere that showcases the landscapes that people call home.[17] Montana is one of the most rural states in the United States, and a fierce pride in the land is one of the most distinguishing characteristics of its residents, so outdoor Shakespeare is a particularly nice fit. Writing a tribute to Bruce Jacobsen when he passed away in 2006, Joel Jahnke reflected that MSIP's founder "was all Montanan and as much of a cowboy as anyone I've met," for "who else would dare to pull into town, set up a ramshackle stage, beat a drum to attract a crowd, put on a play (Shakespeare, no less) and ride out the next day in search of new adventures—leaving behind a group of fascinated locals much richer for the experience?"[18]

The icon that epitomizes MSIP's restless spirit is the road.[19] The alternating romance and monotony of driving all summer long gives rise to imaginative landscapes that are as expansive as the physical ones. Being in a different place for nearly every performance adds to the mystique as well. Jacobsen noted that what struck him most in the first years was the mobility of the production: "Within one hour after we arrived in an area we were ready to start the show. And it took only 45 minutes to pack up and head for home."[20] The increased elaborateness of the set and props has necessitated longer set-up and take-down times in recent years, but notwithstanding, the sense that the actors "are melted into air, into thin air," as Prospero says (4.1.150), is very much part of the tour, along with the Willie Nelson twang of "On the Road Again." When a British-based initiative called Shakespeare on the Road visited North American companies in 2014, MSIP welcomed them with a signpost pointing the direction to a dozen locations on the tour, with the mileage written on each—a deliberate echo of the real sign pointing the way to ranches in the Birney area (see prologue).

Year after year, MSIP photos show the trailer, affectionately called "The Whale," being pulled down expansive roads in wide open countryside, actors posing next to the Ford Expedition, and many other shots that evoke the sense of relentless, and romantic, travel through Montana and surrounding states. Inspired by MSIP's transient schedule, some fans take to the road too, following the company from location to location. Every year a man named Weezel spends a week following the company to various northwest Montana locations, while an annual road trip by a Minnesotan woman and her daughters allows them to return to Montana to see MSIP in the eastern half of the state. The Burroughs family of Bozeman perhaps set the record in 2017 when they saw MSIP perform twenty-six times in seventeen different locations.

Figure 33. MSIP actor James Houton and the company truck near White Sulphur Springs, 2005. Photo courtesy of MSIP archives.

Because of Montana's diverse landscapes, each place holds a challenge and a magic of its own. The backdrop of the play could be a forest, jagged peaks of the Rocky Mountains, a butte, or a dry sagebrush hill. Such radical changes in the landscapes, Pullman noted, were integral to the tour, for "the outdoors became a framing audiovisual that can add a lot of suspense to a plot."[21] Shakespeare's plays regularly reference the weather, the sky, the flora and fauna, so the outdoor locations allow actors to gesture, appropriately or ironically, to the wider setting. Such a literal mise-en-scène makes Shakespeare, for lack of a better term, "natural." The actors, especially before the sound system that was implemented in 2005, endured a vocal challenge unlike any in their careers. The physical demands of being heard required a tremendous amount of energy, but it also created a sense of truly inhabiting the spaces that were filled by these voices. As one reviewer opined, this tour had "no frills. Just a stage, the actors and the spoken word."[22]

Ethnographer Norman Denzin writes that "Montana is both a performance and a place for performances, and it is hardly an innocent stage waiting

Figure 34. The MSIP stage set up for a performance at Makoshika State Park, near Glendive. Photo by Andrew Rathgeber, 2015.

for performances to happen."[23] Denzin's subject in his essay about "performing Montana" is cultural activities such as the mountain men rendezvous and Finn days, but his comments are equally applicable to MSIP—not just because the performances are more foregrounded but because of the ways in which the actors ultimately embrace the parts of the tour that immerse them in the natural environments of Montana. They swim in the Tongue River, climb the badlands of Makoshika State Park, hike the trails of Yellowstone, and sometimes run into bears.

The natural landscape affords breathtaking beauty and some serendipitous moments, but being outside comes with a host of challenges. The *Montana Collegian* reported of the first season: "The Competition included barking dogs, baseball games, mosquitoes, gasoline-powered lawn mowers, trains and occasional thunderstorms."[24] Forty-seven years later, all of these potential distractions, and more, are part of the MSIP experience. Yet of all the aspects of outdoor performance, it is the unpredictable weather that has become like a character in its own right. The meteorological extremes are dramatic: cold rains early in the season, the blistering heat of eastern Montana, hailstorms, wind that carries away the words and blows over set pieces.[25] Actor Brian Massman told of how one year in Birney "an evening thunderstorm forced cast and audience into an abandoned ranch store. People were literally packed to the rafters. . . . There were half a dozen babies crying and the smoke from the battle scene made the confusion worse. . . . It's amazing how people stick with us through cold and freezing weather."[26] Such "weathering" of a play becomes a point of pride for both actors and audience; the 1996 *Clarion* reported that "despite vehicle breakdowns, actor injuries, forest fires, hail storms and an attack squirrel, we didn't lose a show the whole season!" An account of the changing weather is vividly captured in the documentary *Bard in the Backcountry*, where a beautiful, sunny late-afternoon sky above Makoshika State Park in Glendive suddenly gave way to a massive storm that the actors nervously waited out in a tin shed.

Most of the time, such encounters with the elements and the creatures are a vehicle for humorous stories, for the meteorological threats have never caused a serious problem for the actors or audience members. The tour coordinator at Heron in the western part of the state remembers that once a crowd of eight hundred came to see *Comedy of Errors*, but suddenly "our ball park was surrounded by a storm. It was really windy, pouring rain in other parts of Heron. And then when that fellow came out in the play, discussing the storm at sea, there were these thunder claps. People in the back were jumping up and down, waving their arms. The actors thought it was a really enthusiastic crowd, but it was actually that the wind was blowing ants out of the trees! But the show went on."[27] The combination between the action of the play and the natural elements invariably creates a shared experience; audience members cannot help but remember "the time when . . ." the conditions were terrible, but the Shakespeare does indeed go on.

The massive forest fires in Yellowstone in 1988 likewise proved to be no deterrent for the residents of Silver Gate who hosted MSIP that year. When the actors drove to the location, remembers Doug McIntyre, they saw "nothing but smoke and a blood red sun," and there were dozens of firetrucks and firefighters; the telephone poles had even been wrapped with insulated foil.[28] They went on to perform *Merchant of Venice* to a sizable crowd, even while ash settled on the costumes.

Because MSIP is always immersed in the environment of Montana, with all its beauty but also its terrors and vulnerabilities, MSIP productions have proven to be an effective way to explore the negative impact that humans have on the natural world. Asselin's 2014 *As You Like It* was set in 1917 Butte, equating the corrupt court with the Anaconda Copper Mining Company—the corporation whose practices caused such catastrophic environmental impact in that area. The retreat to Arden was an escape to the beauty of a supposedly unspoiled, Edenic Yaak Valley in northwest Montana. Looking forward rather than back, MSIP's 2017 production of *Macbeth* was set in a dystopic future Montana in which society had collapsed because of climate change disaster. The setting, costumes, and sound effects all evoked a world of terror where resources such as water were scarce and the air was poisonous. This concept became eerily relevant as forest fires ripped through the West that year, leaving so much smoke in the air that audience members and actors alike were coughing from the "fog and filthy air" evoked by the witches in the opening scene of the Scottish play.[29] The postapocalyptic landscape allowed an overlay of medieval Scotland, early modern England, and future Montana. The Macbeths' ultimate crimes were against children and regeneration, so this production was able to raise questions about our own responsibility to future generations.[30] Such artistic endeavors echo Denzin's notion of Montana as a liminal place, "a place for new performances, new stories, a place betwixt and between the past and the future. When you are in Montana, you occupy this liminal place, a place that is constantly changing you."[31] Denzin is struck by the limits of words in such a place, but it is interesting to note how often Shakespeare's words succeed where our everyday language fails.

Shakespeare was from a rural area and his plays abound with references to nature—not just its beauty but its dangers and the complicated relationship that humans have with it. Jacobsen's vision for MSIP relied upon the Shakespearean connections to the natural world, for as Jahnke later reflected: "As we travel many of the same old dusty trails that we have been riding now these many summers, [Jacobsen's] pioneer spirit, his love of this land and his dream for making Montana a better place to live rides with us."[32]

Community

Pictures of empty Montana landscapes belie the deeper truth: there are settlements throughout every region of the state. And such places are at the core of

MSIP's mission. When Jacobsen envisioned bringing free Shakespeare to underserved communities, he did not intend to impart a specific kind of book-learning from the university but instead sheer exuberance and fun through theatre. Likewise, Jahnke was dedicated to having fun with Shakespeare, and Asselin continues to emphasize the wonder and magic of theatre. Audiences love these shows, especially relishing moments of shared laughter. When the actors bring this sort of energy to a lawn in a Montana town, they get to know the audiences in a way that simply isn't possible in other kinds of theatrical endeavors.[33]

Presenting Shakespeare free of charge in so many locations is not solely enabled by funding from the state university, grants, and individual donors, for each stop requires local tour coordinators whose significant time and energy make these performances possible. These coordinators raise money for the sponsorship fee, organize the local advertising, arrange for the venue and accommodations, and put together meals for the actors. Because of the tight scheduling that necessitates taking down and packing the set after an evening show, these are often late-night dinners, sometimes followed by early breakfasts before the crew must hit the road again. The way that the actors have been welcomed with the hospitality of food has been noted since the company's earliest days. As Jacobsen wrote in 1977:

> Quite often our appearance is a community social event.... There's a great deal of interaction with the community and it's a very delightful experience to meet these folks. Our actors who often stay in private homes go away raving about the hospitality and warmth they've received as well as the good food—they all gain weight.[34]

In recent years the rigors of the more substantial set and more elaborate props as well as the speakers for the sound system seem to have the opposite effect: actors slim down and gain muscle tone over the summer, and they're always hungry, gratefully eating what the hosts provide (even when it's as unusual as the shoulder of a mountain lion!) and appreciating the way that dietary restrictions are heeded.[35] Eating is a communal activity, so the meal tables create an arena for shared experience and understanding. The very nature of MSIP's performances encourages the audience to eat as well; the usual practice is to bring picnics for family and friends to share over the course of the evening.

MSIP productions invariably include moments when actors break the fourth wall, addressing and even walking through the audience. Usually such moments are designed to heighten comic effect, especially when actors make audience members part of the show. Both the Porter in the 2017 *Macbeth* and Dromio of Ephesus in the 2016 *Comedy of Errors* not only entered the audience but blatantly "stole" food from them. Dromio's hilarious antics (e.g., pouring an entire bag of potato chips into his mouth) made everyone laugh, but they also served as a reminder that a community event such as a play is predicated upon acts of sharing. *Comedy of Errors* is about twinship, and that year when the two Dromios exited the stage speaking of their uncanny resemblance, part of the humor was that they didn't look that much alike. In the fantasy of the play, however, they were in fact twins, just as this shared experience of community Shakespeare temporarily erases the differences between actors from Chicago and ranchers from Glendive.

Difference is the engine of comedy. Shakespeare built his comic moments out of misused words, partially overheard conventions, and mistaken identity. The famous *Twelfth Night* scene (2.5) in which Malvolio picks up a letter that he believes is from Olivia confessing her love for him succeeds because he is being overheard by others who are mocking him for his pretention. This sort of exclusion has dark energy—something explored by Marti Lyons in her 2017 Shakespeare in the Schools *Twelfth Night* production, which focused on the cruel nature of Malvolio's treatment, showing the damage that can be caused by a practical joke taken too far. Yet even when MSIP shows the darker sides of such comedies, they are enacting an opposite mission that can bridge potential divides.

With food and hospitality inevitably come conversation. The community-sponsored arrangements for the actors mean that the play does not end with the curtain call. Actors regularly delight in the discussions they have about the play with the audience afterward. Pullman noted, "It was stunning to me that there was an ability to talk about the text at length"—an assortment of people that might include "a rancher, a teacher, someone who brought kids to the shows," and others.[36] Observations about the intelligent, interested audience are frequent, such as when Jahnke heard two people on Poker Jim Butte debating about the portrayal of Malvolio in two different *Twelfth Night* productions they had seen MSIP do over the years (see prologue). Responding to this description, scholar Susan Bennett wrote, "This audience not only defies an appropriately shaped knowledge of who goes to the theatre, and especially of who goes to see Shakespeare, but perhaps also enjoys a special expertise derived precisely from the intersection of the plays, the performers, and the place."[37] Such audience expertise is an important legacy in Montana, for one can see in the observations about MSIP spectators the same sort of language that was used by Daniel Bandmann a century or more earlier (see chapter 4).

When actors and community members speak of what makes MSIP unique, they evoke the importance of annual ritual and the creation of family.[38] Those actors who tour repeatedly are able to get to know—and even to feel like a part of—extended families. They watch children grow up as the years pass, and sometimes the audience members watch the actors grow up a bit too. The most noted such case was of Great Falls native Mark Kuntz, who saw the shows with his parents throughout his childhood, was brought to MSIP as an acting intern in 1996, and went on to be the company manager for twelve tours—more than any other MSIP actor.[39] The newspapers and the *Clarion* found the story of this young Shakespeare fan turned MSIP company manager irresistible.[40]

Like any family, MSIP sustains its legendary status through storytelling. Every Chicago actor has heard stories about the elements, about the mystic power of Poker Jim Butte, and about Great Falls' mermaid tiki bar called the Sip-n-Dip. And they've also heard about how veteran actor Tom Morris (as Dogberry) incorporated a dog who wandered onstage as part of the play. And about Pullman's production of *A Midsummer Night's Dream* in Miles City in which the cotton from the cottonwood trees fell so thickly that it looked like a snowstorm and got in the actors' mouths. And about the dead owl that ominously fell onto the stage during a musical performance of *Love's Labour's Lost* in Bozeman in 1999. And about the many actors who fell in and out of love, and out and in to tragedy, over the course of the tour and beyond.

Good theatre is about effective storytelling. Shakespeare understood as much, taking an array of well-known plots and characters and weaving them into "yarns" that have remained spellbinding to people in subsequent generations and vastly different regions. The people of Montana seem to have a particular desire to see the transcendence of Shakespearean stories. Perhaps this goes back to an awareness that stories keep people alive. In the long exposition to *Comedy of Errors*, the distraught father Egeus narrates the separation of his family at sea. He's almost like Scheherazade, using the story to preserve his life in a foreign land. Letting Shakespeare's stories speak year after year in some sense also preserves a cultural and communal life in this land called Montana.

Shakespeare's comedies and romances show the miracle of rebirth—those who were thought to be dead are resurrected through art. The conclusion to *Winter's Tale* shows art coming to life as Hermione, the wronged wife of Leontes, poses as a statue of herself sixteen years later, ready to "come to life" through forgiving her husband and reuniting with her family. When Bill Brown directed this play for MSIP in 1998, he wrote that *Winter's Tale* "makes us laugh and it offers us hope. . . . Distance and Time, all-healing Time, prove more powerful than ever."[41] Such forgiveness requires, Shakespeare's play tells us, belief and communal participation, and the result is a magic that is as "lawful as eating" (5.3.111). As art comes to life, it is the stories both within and about MSIP that create community and endure. The common cliché that Shakespeare is "not for an age, but for all time" is true—but that's because of the way he is used to create and recreate stories in vast, unknown landscapes, echoing with "words, words, words."[42]

EPILOGUE

Saved by Shakespeare

It is perchance that you yourself were saved.
—*Twelfth Night*

In 1991, in the midst of the first Gulf War, a young, troubled, and drunk man stumbled off an Amtrak train into Whitefish. He had served in the military for several years and was suffering from the trauma of seeing his best friend killed in a live-fire training exercise. As Stephan Wolfert himself narrates, he disembarked "deep in the Montana mountains" on impulse and wandered into the theatre that was down the street from the depot. When the lights went down for the play, a disabled soldier began with the words "Now is the winter of our discontent / Made glorious summer by this son of York" (*Richard III*, 1.1.1–2). Wolfert was blown away by the connection between broken bodies, spirits, and war as expressed by Shakespeare. He later wrote of this moment, "While watching this deformed, military man, I felt a chromosomal explosion in my body. I writhed in my seat. I jammed heaving sobs back into my mouth only to have them come out louder. I dry heaved while his speech sliced its way directly to my subatomic matter."[1]

This experience inspired him to a life in theatre; Wolfert currently works for a company in New York City called Bedlam that does performance workshops for veterans suffering from PTSD. He has also become well-known for his one-man show called "Cry, Havoc!" (titled after the line from *Julius Caesar*) that tells his story. He always begins with the Amtrak train in Montana and the uncanny salvation through Shakespeare in this state. Although the

Montana setting and the train give this story special power, Wolfert's experience of salvation through Shakespeare strikes a familiar chord. A book called *Shakespeare Saved My Life*,[2] for instance, details one example of a prison education program; such initiatives all over the world have resulted in real and transformative experiences for the inmates who take part.[3]

The Montana State Prison has been in Deer Lodge since 1871. The old prison building still stands, now housing a museum that chronicles its history, including a dark past of prisoner abuse that erupted into a notorious riot in 1959. On the old prison grounds MSIP performs its show annually for the residents of Deer Lodge, bringing entertainment to this small community in the valley where the Stuart brothers once settled, where Laura Honey Agnes Stevenson performed her *Romeo and Juliet* burlesque, where one of the state's first women's clubs was formed, and where Montana's first institution of higher learning was built.[4] Now, however, the economy of the three-thousand-resident Deer Lodge is entirely dependent upon the new prison, which was built in 1979 and houses 1,500 inmates.

In 2015 I codirected a Shakespeare course at this prison—the first and only educational outreach of its kind in Montana. Despite being inspired by books, papers, and documentaries about Shakespeare in prison programs, I was reluctant to walk into the Deer Lodge prison assuming that I was presenting Shakespeare as a path to salvation. What made this program unique, however, is that my coteacher was Zach Stenberg, who was both an MSU honors student finishing up his English literature degree and a former inmate at that facility. During his nine-year incarceration, he had discovered reading, devouring hundreds of books that completely altered his outlook and quite literally did save his life.

We taught sixteen men *The Tempest*, *Macbeth*, and *Hamlet* in that course, and I am certain that I learned far more than my students did. The raw, personal way they approached these stories made it the most meaningful teaching experience of my life. Prospero's question of forgiveness was vital; Hamlet's metaphor about Denmark being a prison was literalized; and Macbeth's nightmare of killing on impulse and staring at his blood-covered hands was chillingly apt. Each student had his own story, but they all found an uncanny connection to a four-hundred-year-old British playwright. The participants memorized soliloquies and recited them with an honesty all their own.

On the first night, the course participants introduced themselves, one by one. As they gave their names, they each used a turn of phrase I had never heard before: "I fell from Great Falls . . . ," "I fell from Miles City . . . ," "I fell from Kalispell . . . ." This was their way of identifying the place in Montana where they were arrested. The language of the "fall" seemed to beg for salvation, but while the program was successful in a variety of ways, I can't say that I have a story in which Shakespeare saved anyone's life. What I remember most clearly, however, is the moment when I returned later in the year to teach *The Winter's Tale*, and a young man asked me about the break between Act 3 and Act 4 of the play. At the beginning of Act 4 an allegorical representation of Time announces that sixteen years have passed, lived in darkness for King Leontes, who has so heinously wronged his family and friends. "Wait a minute, what happened to those years?," asked the nineteen-year-old who was facing the possibility of another seventy years behind bars. The years had been swallowed up, devoured by Time. I had no words of my own for that haunted prisoner, so I could only offer what seems to impact people the most: stories of Shakespeare. While there is no way to retrieve such loss, *Winter's Tale* does allow for the possibility of reconciliation and life on the other side of the chasm.

Shakespeare resonates in countless ways in Montana's long history and throughout its diverse landscapes. But he's always there—sometimes as the goal toward which the sojourners deliberately travel, sometimes as the unexpected destination, but always interwoven into history, lore, and the imagination of the frontier.

NOTES

Preface

1. Cooper, *Notions of the Americans*, 2:148.
2. Vaughan and Vaughan, *Shakespeare in America*, 72. Similar arguments have been made in Shapiro, *Shakespeare in America*, and Sturgess, *Shakespeare and the American Nation*.
3. The most widely read and cited accounts of Shakespeare in the American West are van Orman, "Bard in the West"; Carrell, "How the Bard Won the West"; Davidson, "Shakespeare in the Rockies"; and Greenwald, "Rough-Hewn Stages."
4. Carrell, "How the Bard Won the West." See also Levine, *Highbrow/Lowbrow*.
5. Weiland and Wilsey, *State by State*, 263.
6. Denzin, "Performing Montana," 158.
7. Gaunt's speech is not merely an homage to his precious land of England, for it ends with a lament that the land "is now leased out," for England "Hath made a shameful conquest of itself" (*Richard II*, 2.1.66).

Prologue

1. Jahnke interview.
2. There are just over a million people in Montana, spread over 147,000 square miles, which makes it the third least densely populated state. Considering the geographical distance and isolation of many communities in the state, the scope of MSIP's outreach is all the more remarkable.
3. The documentary *Bard in the Backcountry*, which follows the actors over the course of a summer season to capture the essence of the tour and the company, also devotes its opening sequence to Poker Jim Butte.
4. Margie Fjell Knobloch reminisces about that time: "We had lots of fun, lots of relatives, and lots of just people around Birney.... Our community center was the Corell Bar. We had movies and dances and any social gatherings—that is

where they did it. And they had wonderful dances. People came from all over the country to come to the dances at Birney." Knobloch, "Cultural Landscape of the Upper Tongue River Valley."

5. *Backroads of Montana.*
6. Walton correspondence.
7. For quite a few years Forrest Mars Jr., heir to the Mars confectionery company, sponsored MSIP's performance in Birney, though he apparently never attended. In 2012 he sold the Diamond Cross Ranch, leaving the MSIP Poker Jim Butte performance without an underwriter.
8. Walton correspondence.
9. McRae, *Stick Horses*, 127.
10. Mary Cochrane McIvor, "Pullman & Shakespeare in Montana," June 3, 2002, https://www.billpullman.org/bp_montanashkspinparks.
11. *Billings Gazette*, September 29, 1937.
12. Richards correspondence.
13. *Bard in the Backcountry*, chap. 6.
14. Smith interview. Bill Brown, whose first tour was in 1980, was convinced that this was a joke that they played on the rookies, driving them up to this isolated place and claiming that people were going to appear to see Shakespeare. *Bard in the Backcountry* supplementary interview.
15. Jahnke interview.
16. Dickerson interview.
17. "About Shakespeare in the Parks," Montana Shakespeare in the Parks, http://www.shakespeareintheparks.org/about/overview.
18. Reierson correspondence.
19. Western novelist Louis L'Amour also described this landscape: "At the top of the ridge I looked back across at the Hanging Woman [Creek] toward Poker Jim Butte and the Otter Creek country. You never saw anything more peaceful than that spread of land right then, but I was not a trusting man." L'Amour, *Hanging Woman Creek*, chap. 5.
20. *Backroads of Montana.*
21. Asselin interview.
22. Jahnke interview. He likewise narrated this story for the *New York Times* in 2004. Jim Robbins, "In Montana, Shakespeare in the Sky," *New York Times*, July 18, 2004.
23. McRae, *Stick Horses*, 128.
24. McRae, 132.
25. *Backroads of Montana.*
26. Morris interview.
27. Smith interview.
28. Foss correspondence.
29. The popular movie phrase from *Field of Dreams* (1989)—"If you build it, they will come"—is also evoked in *Backroads of Montana.*

30. Hagen interview.

31. Poker Jim Butte embodies Jeff Malpas's notion of places, which "are a curious combination of lived experience and imagination, memory included." Malpas, *Intelligence of Place*, 54.

32. Lucy R. Lippard, quoted in Malpas, 52.

33. *Antony and Cleopatra*, 3.13.47.

Chapter 1

1. Russell, *Journal of a Trapper*, 109.

2. Russell, 54.

3. Victor, *River of the West*, 84.

4. Will Cave, "First 'Show' in Montana," *Missoulian*, March 26, 1922, quoted in Porter, "Compilation of Materials," 7.

5. Victor, *River of the West*, 84.

6. Tocqueville, *Democracy in America*, 538.

7. As Vaughan and Vaughan demonstrate, during the late eighteenth and early nineteenth centuries, Shakespeare was not, in fact, a cornerstone of American education. Vaughan and Vaughan, *Shakespeare in America*, 79.

8. Hamilton, *My Sixty Years on the Plains*, 46.

9. The Gore expedition was in the Tongue River area of Montana, not far from Poker Jim Butte (see prologue).

10. Marcy, *Thirty Years of Army Life*, 403.

11. Carrington, *Ab-sa-ra-ka*, 114.

12. Humfreville, *Twenty Years among Our Hostile Indians*, 404.

13. Humfreville, 404.

14. See Alter, *Jim Bridger*, 302.

15. Stuart, *Forty Years on the Frontier*, 159–61.

16. Stuart, *Diary and Sketchbook*, 9. See *Hamlet*, 1.4.14–15.

17. Stuart, 10.

18. *New York Times*, June 13, 1926.

19. Bourke, *On the Border with Crook*, 299.

20. Fayette W. Roe, Scrapbook (1870), History Museum Archives, Great Falls, Montana.

21. Stiles, *Custer's Trials*, 136.

22. Warhank, "Fort Keogh," 266–67.

23. Adams, *Class and Race in the Frontier Army*, 37, and n26. See also *Yellowstone Journal and Live Stock Reporter*, May 10, 1884.

24. Quoted in Fayette W. Roe, Scrapbook (1870), History Museum Archives, Great Falls, Montana. See *Merchant of Venice*, 5.1.85.

25. Milner and O'Connor, *As Big as the West*, 289.

26. Vaughan and Vaughan, *Shakespeare in America*, 30. See also Ambrose, who contends that, based on references in Lewis's writings, one can infer that he read "a

little ancient history, some Milton and Shakespeare, and a smattering of recent British history." Ambrose, *Undaunted Courage*, 28.

27. Stephen Ambrose says that Clark gave a set of Shakespeare to his teenage bride (*Undaunted Courage*, 460), but Stephenie Ambrose Tubbs says it was Lewis. (Tubbs, "Clark, Judith Hancock," in *Lewis and Clark Companion*).

28. Sammye Meadows, cultural awareness coordinator for the National Council of the Lewis and Clark Bicentennial's Circle of Tribal Elders, called Jean Baptiste "the Shakespeare-quoting mountain man . . . completely at home in the wilderness and also completely at home in aristocratic European culture." Quoted in *Billings Gazette*, July 8, 2006.

29. Frances Hunter, "Sacagawea's Boy: The Story of Pomp," *Frances Hunter's American Heroes Blog*, December 1, 2009, https://franceshunter.wordpress.com/2009/12/01/sacagaweas-boy-the-story-of-pomp. See also *Billings Gazette*, July 8, 2006.

30. See the account of Maungwudaus's visit on the Shakespeare Birthplace Trust website: Norma Hampson, "Chief Maungwudaus Visits the Birthplace in 1848," *Explore Shakespeare* (blog), Shakespeare Birthplace Trust, July 28, 2014, https://www.shakespeare.org.uk/explore-shakespeare/blogs/chief-maungwudaus-visits-birthplace-1848/.

Interlude 1

1. Wister, *Virginian*, 120.
2. Wister, 217.
3. See Stanley and Thatcher, *Cowboy Poets and Cowboy Poetry*.
4. Noyes, *In the Land of Chinook*, 50.
5. Rollins, *Cowboy*, 128.
6. *Livingston Enterprise*, July 10, 1886.
7. *A Midsummer Night's Dream*, 3.1.203.
8. Greenfield, "Shakespearean 'Culture' in Montana," 50, 53–54.
9. Rod Miller, "Opening the Gates," *Featured at the Bar-D Ranch* (blog), Western and Cowboy Poetry, Music & More at the Bar-D Ranch, http://www.cowboypoetry.com/gates.htm#gates.

Chapter 2

1. Quotations from *1 Henry IV*, 5.3.201, and *Hamlet*, 1.5.28.
2. *Measure for Measure*, 2.2.179–80.
3. *Macbeth*, 2.2.61–62 (though Dimsdale omits the word "great" before "Neptune's") and *Hamlet*, 3.3.37, respectively.
4. *Vigilantes* was published in book form in 1866, and it was the first book to be published in Montana Territory.
5. Speaking of this edition, Dunn posits, "Probably never since Shakespeare's own day had his plays been so gaily handled." Dunn, *Shakespeare in America*, 287.

6. See *Montana Post*, July 21, 1866. Some accounts give the location of the restaurant as Idaho Street.

7. Blake, "Memoirs of a Many-Sided Man," 47–48.

8. *Montana Post*, September 3, 1864. As Carrell notes, the West is full of mines with Shakespearean names, such as Ophelia, Cordelia, Desdemona, and even Timon. Carrell, "How the Bard Won the West."

9. For the role of "hurdy-gurdy girls" in Bannack, see Lowe, *Bannack*, 4–5.

10. Malone, Roeder, and Lang, *Montana*, 68.

11. In *Pioneer Trails and Trials*, 854. See *Macbeth*, I.I.I.

12. The program is held by the Bannack State Park archives. The son and daughter of Hezekiah Hosmer would have been respectively fourteen and eleven years old in 1864. This *Edward IV* program notes that the performance starred J. A. (John Allen) Hosmer and Miss S. E. (Sarah Elizabeth) Hosmer.

13. *Montana Post*, November 26, 1864.

14. Cochran, "Gold Dust Trail," 64. The caption from a Montana Historical Society photo of the People's Theatre notes that it was described by a *New York Tribune* correspondent as "a hall, capable of holding two hundred and fifty persons, with a rude little rear gallery, long wooden benches, and a great wood stove, an orchestra of four, five tallow candles, for footlights, a green cambric drop curtain and a stage the size of a small bedroom."

15. *Montana Post*, May 19, 1866.

16. Nealy, "A Year in Montana." Apparently Nealy thought the vaudeville and minstrel shows more "legitimate" entertainment in the Rockies' mining camps. The phrase "Othello's occupation's gone" (*Othello*, 3.3.360) is frequently employed in the newspapers of the period to refer to the loss of status or political clout. One parody in the *Montana Post* used this as the opening line of a description of a territorial legislative meeting (April 15, 1865).

17. *Montana Post*, November 3, 1866.

18. Levine, "William Shakespeare and the American People," 163.

19. Lauterbach and Lauterbach, *Comedian of the Frontier*, 99.

20. *Montana Post*, December 21, 1867.

21. *Montana Post*, December 21, 1867. The reviewer also complains that "Mrs. Fitzwilliams was not in her most happy vein as Desdemona."

22. See Cochran, "Jack Langrishe and Theater," 56, for more about the *Montana Post* critics' disapproval of Pauncefort.

23. Koon, *How Shakespeare Won the West*, 11–12. She also notes that "the average miner was between twenty and thirty years old, had at least a sixth grade education, and was familiar with Shakespeare, either because he had learned long passages from McGuffey's Reader or had seen a traveling theater company. He might even have played in an amateur production" (3–4).

24. *Montana Post*, September 7, 1867. The following week the newspaper reported that "Mrs. Langrishe met with a painful accident" when "in passing through the theater before it was lit up, she struck her foot against a piece of timber

dislocating a joint," which caused her to miss her second performance (*Montana Post*, September 14, 1867).

25. See Barsness, *Gold Camp*, 228.

26. The Virginia City Players performed a *Romeo and Juliet* spoof in the 1950s (Hanisch, *Stage Presence*, 6). The Vigilante Theatre Company, which was based in Dillon and Bozeman from 1981 to 2013, came out of a similar theatrical tradition as the Virginia City Players, but the Vigilantes toured all over the state, performing original plays such as "The Clark and Lewis Show," "History Mystery Train," and "Adventures on a Western Stage." Hosking, interview. See also *Bozeman Daily Chronicle*, July 20, 2013.

27. See Cochran, "Gold Dust Trail," 66–67. Cochran also asserts that "Shakespeare, melodrama, and farce appealed to the miner who, unwashed and uncombed, could relax after a hard day's digging and reassure himself that he was not becoming a barbarian, that he was in but not of his grubby environment" (61).

28. Greever, *Bonanza West*, 231.

29. This opera house was built in 1870 but burned to the ground in 1874.

30. *Montana Post*, July 17, 1868.

31. The Langrishe company staged a *Macbeth* that was notable for its exaggerated witch scenes: the actors uttered "weird incantations . . . with full choruses," and they were "as diabolical looking hags as ever felt their thumbs prick at the approach of evil." *Montana Post*, December 14, 1867.

32. *Central City Weekly Register-Call*, December 13, 1895.

33. Ogden, *Theatre West*, 110.

34. Some thought, in fact, that Langrishe's talents as an actor were limited. The *Montana Mountaineer* (Marysville) described him as "a large man with a big nose and homely face, and a poor actor" who was nonetheless "very popular among the rough miners." Quoted in Lauterbach and Lauterbach, *Comedian of the Frontier*, 218.

35. Cochran, "Jack Langrishe and Theater," 48.

36. Thomas Bowdler, from whose name the term *bowdlerized* derives, published *The Family Shakespeare* in 1807, but many others throughout the nineteenth century also produced heavily edited versions of the plays.

37. Lauterbach and Lauterbach, *Comedian of the Frontier*, 216.

38. *Montana Post*, September 28, 1867.

39. Lauterbach and Lauterbach, *Comedian of the Frontier*, 103.

40. Lauterbach and Lauterbach, 174.

41. Cochran, "Jack Langrishe and Theater," 49. Quoted from *Rocky Mountain News*, September 14, 1883.

42. See *Macbeth*, 5.5.24–25.

43. Quoted in Lauterbach and Lauterbach, *Comedian of the Frontier*, 218. See *1 Henry IV*, 5.4.101–3.

44. McClure, *Three Thousand Miles*, 409.

45. *Montana Post*, January 12, 1867.

46. McClure, *Three Thousand Miles*, 409.

47. Ellen Baumler, "The Women of Virginia City Tour," *Women's History Matters* (blog), Montana Historical Society, http://montanawomenshistory.org/wp-content/uploads/2015/04/Women-of-VA-City_TourMap.pdf, 2.

48. Ronan and Ronan, *Girl from the Gulches*, 19.

49. Ronan and Ronan, 52.

50. Ronan and Ronan, 58; *Hamlet*, 2.2.539. Mary married Peter Ronan, who served as the government agent to the Flathead Reservation from 1877 to 1893.

51. Andrew Dickson, "West Side Story: How Shakespeare Stormed America's Frontier," *Guardian*, April 15, 2016, https://www.theguardian.com/stage/2016/apr/15/william-shakespeare-american-west-pioneers.

52. See Behan, "Forgotten Heritage."

53. This reaction in Virginia City was no doubt due to the large percentage of Virginia City residents who came from the South. Mary was, nonetheless, punished by her parents for joining in this celebration of the assassination.

54. *Macbeth* was in fact Lincoln's favorite play, and it is tempting to read this fascination as a foreshadowing of his assassination. See Beran, "Lincoln, *Macbeth*, and the Moral Imagination," for more on the Lincoln-Macbeth connection.

55. *Montana Post*, July 5, 1866.

56. This song is from *A Midsummer Night's Dream*, 2.1.

57. "The Miners' Juliet," *Iola Register*, July 24, 1879. For the biography of Stevenson and the many versions of her story, see "Stevenson, Laura Agnes," Simon Fraser University Digitized Collections, digital.lib.sfu.ca/ceww-716/Stevenson-laura-agnes.

58. *Anaconda Standard*, October 23, 1898 (article by John Maguire).

59. "The Miners' Juliet," *Iola Register*, July 24, 1879.

60. C. C. Clawson, "*Romeo and Juliet* in the Far West," *New York Clipper*, December 7, 1878.

61. *Anaconda Standard*, October 23, 1898 (article by John Maguire).

62. C. C. Clawson, "*Romeo and Juliet* in the Far West," *New York Clipper*, December 7, 1878.

63. "The Miners' Juliet," *Iola Register*, July 24, 1879.

64. *Anaconda Standard*, October 23, 1898 (article by John Maguire).

65. *Kendall Miner*, March 12, 1909. See *Hamlet*, 1.5.27.

66. Judge DeKalb, "Review of the History of Lewistown," August 16, 1949, Lewistown Public Library, Lewistown, Montana.

67. *Kendall Miner*, March 18, 1906 (though this ad was reprinted throughout that year). See *A Midsummer Night's Dream*, 2.1.249 (the quotation in the original is: "I know a bank where the wild thyme blows").

Interlude 2

1. See chapter 2. The *Butte Miner* (May 20, 1883) also prints an account of Miss

Hosmer's entertainment at the Renshaw Opera House, including recitation of a scene from *Much Ado about Nothing*.

2. In his introduction, Hosmer asserts that the sonnets "were written by Lord Bacon with the intention of disclosing, through the various forms of analogy, allegory, metaphor, and symbolism, all the real facts concerning the composition of the works attributed to Shakespeare." Hosmer, *Bacon and Shakespeare in the Sonnets*, 13.
3. Barsness, *Gold Camp*, 93.
4. One of Hosmer's letters to Twain, asking for help for his friend who was unjustly accused, is preserved in the Montana Historical Society archives in Helena.
5. Twain claims to have published this work, but he apparently changed his mind and then criticized his partner for not doing so. Shapiro, *Contested Will*, 120.
6. *Butte Daily Post*, September 7, 1893. On this occasion Donnelly also spoke against the Free Silver movement (which advocated the unlimited coinage of silver).
7. Shapiro, *Contested Will*, 124.
8. Shapiro, 125.
9. *Missoula Weekly Gazette*, June 10, 1891.
10. Conspiracy theories, however, continue to make for popular stories (consider *A Beautiful Mind, Conspiracy Theory*, and *The Da Vinci Code*, among other books and movies).
11. *Helena Weekly Herald*, March 1, 1888.
12. *Anaconda Standard*, March 25, 1899.
13. *Anaconda Standard*, March 25, 1899.
14. He goes on to say, "And I have less patience with the eloquence of an [Robert Green] Ingersoll that would elevate those ideals to a towering height above the Savior of mankind."
15. *Anaconda Standard*, March 28, 1898.
16. The film *Anonymous* (2011), directed by Roland Emmerich, was an attempt to support the theory that Edward de Vere authored the works attributed to Shakespeare. Like the Bacon theories, this "Oxfordian" film was interested in the scandal surrounding the author of these works and Elizabeth I, thus portrayed de Vere's dual position as lover and son to the Queen.
17. Fellows tells this story in her 2006 book *The Shakespeare Code*, which was published by Summit University Press.
18. Fellows, *Shakespeare Code*, xv.
19. See *Montreal Gazette*, August 22, 1998.
20. Fellows, *Shakespeare Code*, xviii.
21. *Bozeman Magazine*, April 2019.

Chapter 3

1. Albertson, "History of Shakespeare Club," 585.
2. "According to the census, in 1870 Montana had eight men for every one

woman. By 1910, only 39 percent of Montana's population was female. Even in the growing urban centers like Butte, Helena, and Missoula women were relatively rare." Tubbs, "Turn-of-the-Century Women's Clubs," 6.

3. Croly, *History of the Women's Club Movement*, 767.
4. Christie, "Women's Clubs of Montana," 587.
5. Deer Lodge Club history, Kohrs Memorial Library, Deer Lodge, Montana.
6. Butte was one of the first cities in the United States to have electricity (see chapter 4).
7. *Butte Daily Post*, October 2, 1903.
8. See *Much Ado about Nothing*, 2.1.252.
9. Scheil, *She Hath Been Reading*, 80.
10. Fortnightly Club, Montana Historical Society, Helena, Montana. Greenfield also noted that the Shakespeare Club of Great Falls had members who "yearned for eastern culture, either because they missed what they had known or wanted to acquire what they had never known." Greenfield, "Shakespearean 'Culture' in Montana," 49.
11. *Butte Miner*, February 4, 1900.
12. West Side Shakespeare Club minutes, 1910–1911, Butte-Silver Bow Archives, Butte, Montana; and Deer Lodge Club minutes, 1890, Kohrs Memorial Library, Deer Lodge, Montana.
13. Fortnightly Club program, Montana Historical Society, Helena, Montana.
14. Dillon Shakespeare Club history, Dillon Shakespeare Club private collection.
15. West Side Shakespeare Club bylaws, 4.7, Butte-Silver Bow Archives, Butte, Montana.
16. The only play I've never seen mentioned is *Titus Andronicus*, which is in keeping with the nearly universal tendency to ignore this play in the nineteenth century.
17. Other books in the Dillon Shakespeare Club library included Sadakichi Hartmann's *Shakespeare in Art*, Orie Hatcher's *A Book for Shakespeare Plays and Pageants*, and Ernest Law's *Shakespeare's Garden*.
18. In A. T. Quiller-Couch's *Historical Tales from Shakespeare* (1900), one reader liberally underlined the chapters about Henry IV and Henry V. This sort of research was standard preparation for the presentations that women gave at club meetings, providing historical background to the plays on their program.
19. West Side Shakespeare Club minutes, March 18, 1899, Butte-Silver Bow Archives, Butte, Montana; and As You Like It Club minutes, March 19, 1907, Mansfield Library, University of Montana, Missoula.
20. Ladies' Reading Circle minutes, March 2, 1893, McNulty, Flora McKay, Papers (1872–1938), Montana Historical Society, Helena, Montana.
21. Scheil, *She Hath Been Reading*, 82. Blood purity is also emphasized in McNulty's answer: it was important that Mary Arden traced her roots back to the Anglo-Saxons.
22. *Butte Daily Inter-mountain*, March 29, 1902. This article by a club member

immediately follows one entitled "Laws Affecting Women"—a contemporary consideration of how women are treated that dovetails with the subsequent reflections upon Desdemona.

23. Fortnightly Club minutes, 1892, Montana Historical Society, Helena, Montana; and West Side Shakespeare Club minutes, 1900–1902, Butte-Silver Bow Archives, Butte, Montana.

24. West Side Shakespeare Club programs, 1900–1901, 1904–1905, Butte-Silver Bow Archives, Butte, Montana.

25. Fortnightly Club minutes, November 7, 1896, and December 5, 1896, Montana Historical Society, Helena, Montana.

26. West Side Shakespeare Club Yearbook, 1916–1917, Butte-Silver Bow Archives, Butte, Montana.

27. West Side Shakespeare Club minutes, January 16, 1917, Butte-Silver Bow Archives, Butte, Montana.

28. West Side Shakespeare Club minutes, 1909–1910, Butte-Silver Bow Archives, Butte, Montana; see also Yellowstone Club history, 6, Montana Historical Society, Helena, Montana.

29. Interest in this play was common in women's clubs: "Writing in 1907, Annette Meakin observed that Ibsen's *Doll's House* has 'shown the world that motherhood, even though it be woman's most sacred duty, can never more be looked upon as her final destiny.'" Gere, *Intimate Practices*, 231.

30. Unfortunately, the actress's performance was disappointing, and for some time after the club women were teased that their taste in theatre could not be trusted. Yellowstone Club history, 6, Montana Historical Society, Helena, Montana.

31. The *Daily Missoulian* boasted that "Missoula will give Ellen Terry as good and as royal a welcome as Los Angeles, San Francisco, Spokane, or any of the larger sister cities" (December 10, 1910).

32. *Daily Missoulian*, December 16, 1910.

33. *Missoulian*, December 14, 1910.

34. Ethel Picton, "110 Years of Shakespeare Club," Dillon Shakespeare Club private collection.

35. This club was formed in 1902 by twenty-six "bright, broad-minded women" and included six subdivisions: music, art, literature, domestic/social sciences, Shakespeare, and civic. Mansfield Library, University of Montana, Missoula.

36. Hamilton Woman's Club minutes, February 11, 1918, Montana Historical Society, Helena, Montana.

37. Van Orman, "Bard in the West," 37–38.

38. Gere sees the practice of reading aloud as deviant because "clubwomen could hide under the protective coloring of domestic practices that had emerged earlier in the nineteenth century in response to social concern about the dangerous delights of solitary reading for women." Gere, *Intimate Practices*, 149.

39. Greenfield, "Shakespearean 'Culture' in Montana," 49.

40. *Dillon Tribune*, April 4, 1902.

41. *Dillon Examiner*, April 9, 1902.

42. Dillon Shakespeare Club event program, April 21, 1899, Dillon Shakespeare Club private collection. See also Eliel, *Southwestern Montana*, 74–75, and Christie, "Women's Clubs of Montana," 589.

43. *Anaconda Standard*, April 30, 1899. See *Othello*, 3.3.90–92.

44. *Semi-weekly Billings Gazette*, May 3, 1904.

45. Eliel, *Southwestern Montana*, 75.

46. Greenfield, "Shakespearean 'Culture' in Montana," 53–54.

47. Scheil, *She Hath Been Reading*, 83.

48. Describing the inconvenience of the natural elements at the 1913 suffragette convention in Livingston, one woman wrote that participants rode in "cabs, buggies, wagons and even hayracks," but "it was up to the hostesses to walk. It had rained in the meantime, and picture . . . this unusual sight—plodding through the mud." Yellowstone Club history, 9, Montana Historical Society, Helena, Montana.

49. Quoted in Marra, *Strange Duets*, 97.

50. Quoted in Tubbs, "Turn-of-the-Century Women's Clubs," 12.

51. *Montana Woman* 4, no. 3 (1927). The Teapot Dome scandal itself erupted in 1924, but this article came on the heels of a 1927 Supreme Court ruling that the oil leases had been obtained illegally by Warren Harding's administration.

52. See *Macbeth*, 4.1.

53. Erskine, *Memory of Certain Persons*, 367–68.

54. *Montana Federation of Women's Clubs*, 16.

55. Dillon Shakespeare Club history, Dillon Shakespeare Club private collection.

56. Helena Woman's Club minutes, 1913–1914, Montana Historical Society, Helena, Montana. The words are taken from Thomas Heywood's *An Apology for Actors* (1612).

Interlude 3

1. Professor Carl Holiday spoke on "Shakespeare as a Man" and Percy Stone on "Shakespeare, the Universal." See *Missoulian*, April 27, 1916.

2. *Butte Miner*, April 2, 1916. Speakers included Chancellor Elliot of Missoula, Rabbi Wittenberg, Harold Law, and Carl Holiday.

3. *Butte Miner*, April 2, 1916.

4. *Anaconda Standard*, April 16, 1916.

5. *Anaconda Standard*, April 4, 1916.

6. *Butte Miner*, April 18, 1916.

7. Victor Records ran this ad in newspapers across the country.

8. The Paul Clark Home was dedicated by mining mogul William Clark in memory of his son Paul.

9. *Butte Miner*, April 23, 1916.

10. *Mountaineer*, Butte High School, 1916, 56, Montana Memory Project, mtmemory.org.

11. *Glasgow Courier*, May 19, 1916.

12. *Great Falls Tribune*, March 12, 1916.

13. This is not to say, of course, that all Montana voices were represented. The *Anaconda Standard* published a picture and brief story with the caption "Indian students, in quaint costumes of old, play Shakespeare," which reported that to observe the tercentenary students at the Carlisle Indian School in Pennsylvania "honored the bard with an elaborately costumed presentation of his leading characters in appropriate verse and song before an audience of students and town people." According to the newspaper, these "copper colored Indian youths and maidens" engaged in an "Indian Shakespeare celebration was a tribute to the hitherto almost unsuspected powers of dramatic characterization possessed by the aborigines" (*Anaconda Standard*, June 1, 1916). Such attitudes toward Native Americans performing Shakespeare are of course full of racial stereotypes and discrimination, but it is interesting that there was no analogous move to incorporate the Montana Native population into the tercentenary celebrations.

14. *Butte Miner*, April 2, 1916.

15. Shakespeare400 website, http://www.shakespeare400.org/.

Chapter 4

1. Clark, "John Maguire," 35.

2. Maguire went so far as to copy Belasco in wearing a clerical collar.

3. Maguire's opera houses were in Anaconda, Bozeman, Butte, Deer Lodge, Great Falls, Helena, and Missoula.

4. *Helena Weekly Herald*, September 25, 1884.

5. *Butte Semi-weekly Miner*, June 26, 1889.

6. Some sources say Bandmann's birth year was 1840.

7. *Independent-Record*, May 15, 1884.

8. Coleman, "Daniel E. Bandmann," 35.

9. A Helena newspaper reported: "Maguire's new opera house in Missoula is just completed. It is arranged for seating 600 persons, having a parquette containing 350 chairs. The building will be dedicated as a Temple of the Drama by Herr Bandmann on the 5th of June." *Independent-Record*, May 24, 1884.

10. Coleman, "Daniel E. Bandmann," 32–34. The original text appeared in the *Butte Miner*, December 21, 1902.

11. Coleman, "Daniel E. Bandmann," 36.

12. *Anaconda Standard*, July 10, 1897.

13. Kim Briggeman and Marcia Porter, "Daniel Edward Bandmann," ftp://ftp.ci.missoula.mt.us/Documents/Cemetery/Biographies/BANDMANN,%20Daniel.pdf.

14. In Cormac McCarthy's Western epic *Blood Meridian*, there is a parallel

description of eclectic clothing, but this time it is worn by the Native peoples: "A legion of horribles, hundreds in number, half naked or clad in costumes attic or biblical or wardrobed out of a fevered dream with the skins of animals and silk finery and pieces of uniform still tracked with the blood of prior owners, coats of slain dragoons, frogged and braided cavalry jackets, one in a stovepipe hat and one with an umbrella and one in white stockings and a bloodstained weddingveil." McCarthy, *Blood Meridian*, 55.

15. There was an award established at University of Montana in his honor, called the Daniel E. Bandmann Achievement Award for Outstanding Success in All Phases of Theatre. Students were receiving this award up through the end of the 1960s.

16. *Anaconda Standard*, December 16, 1900.

17. *New York Times*, November 25, 1905.

18. Coleman, "Daniel E. Bandmann," 29

19. *Anaconda Standard*, September 5, 1899.

20. *Missoula Weekly Gazette*, January 27, 1892.

21. Warde, *Fifty Years of Make-Believe*, 222.

22. See *Hamlet*, 1.5.161.

23. Warde, *Fifty Years of Make-Believe*, 223.

24. Warde, 224.

25. *Bozeman Magazine*, February 1, 2017 (article by Cindy Shearer).

26. *Great Falls Tribune*, May 12, 1894.

27. *Butte Daily Inter-mountain*, March 24, 1899.

28. *Dillon Tribune*, April 18, 1902.

29. Desdemona's stabbing is part of John Bell's "acting" version of Shakespeare's plays (1774).

30. *Anaconda Standard*, September 2, 1900.

31. *Anaconda Standard*, August 2, 1900.

32. Other accounts similarly note the large percentage of people who went to Shakespearean performances; when Modjeska performed as Constance in *King John* in 1901, the newspaper noted, "Every Shakespearian reader in Butte occupied a seat in the Grand last night, which is tantamount to saying that the theater was filled from pit to gallery." *Butte Daily Post*, April 19, 1901.

33. *Anaconda Standard*, July 29, 1900.

34. *Butte Miner*, February 4, 1900.

35. *Butte Daily Inter-mountain*, January 26, 1901.

36. *Yellowstone Monitor*, May 25, 1911.

37. *Butte Daily Post*, September 24, 1901. See *Julius Caesar*, 5.5.69.

38. *Anaconda Standard*, April 2, 1894.

39. *Anaconda Standard*, April 1, 1894.

40. Professor Frank Fouche and Henrietta Moore were other elocutionists who traveled widely through Montana.

41. *Great Falls Tribune*, April 28, 1901.

42. The opening lines of Sonnet 29 read: "When, in disgrace with fortune and men's eyes, / I all alone beweep my outcast state, / And trouble deaf heaven with my bootless cries, / And look upon myself, and curse my fate."
43. *Butte Daily Inter-mountain*, March 1, 1902.
44. *Billings Gazette*, April 26, 1908.
45. In 1913 the Dillon paper encouraged people to see "the best films that have ever been made" in their local movie house; titles included *Othello*, *Julius Caesar*, and *Antony and Cleopatra*.
46. Warde went on to play the title role in a *King Lear* film in 1916, but his greatest impact on the medium was probably his "discovery" of Douglas Fairbanks, who acted with Warde's company for several years (1899–1901).
47. *Great Falls Tribune*, November 16, 1916.
48. *Glasgow Courier*, April 12, 1918.
49. *Great Falls Tribune*, March 23, 1923.
50. *Great Falls Tribune*, March 23, 1923.
51. A similar doubt was raised in a Butte paper: "Whether the times are 'out of joint' so far as Shakespeare is concerned, or many modern-day audiences deem Shakespearean plot too turgid, phraseology too rotund, action too much impeded by soliloquy." *Butte Miner*, March 21, 1923.
52. *Missoulian*, March 23, 1923.

Interlude 4

1. According to the protagonist, Morrie, he chooses this phrase from *A Midsummer Night's Dream* because he is seeking "something that carries the sound of promise, that resonates across the land, that dramatically bespeaks the coming clash with Anaconda [the mining company]." Doig, *Sweet Thunder*, 46.
2. *Producers News*, June 20, 1919.
3. *Producers News*, May 9, 1919. This phrase from *Romeo and Juliet* (2.6.9) is frequently quoted in *Westworld*, an HBO series (2016–2020) based on a 1973 Michael Crichton film. The series is set in a science fiction Wild West–themed amusement park inhabited by robots, including a Shakespeare-quoting character called "The Professor."
4. *Producers News*, June 6, 1919.
5. Unfortunately, no records regarding the readings or activities of these Shakespeare departments seem to be extant.
6. *Othello*, 5.2.7.
7. *Julius Caesar*, 4.3.216–19. Washington delivered this address before the national Negro Business League (Chicago, August 22, 1912). At this time he also alluded to *Merchant of Venice*: "These efforts will be twice blessed—blessing 'him that gives and him that takes'" (4.1.183).
8. *Anaconda Standard*, March 5, 1911.
9. Dunbar Art and Study Club ledger, 1922, Montana Historical Society archives.

10. The quotation in the ledger book is from Henry Harrison Brown's poem "Opportunity" about this same *Julius Caesar* quotation: "I pondered long o'er Shakespeare's lines / About a tide in every life / Which, taken full, to victory leads; / Neglected, ends in shallows rife. / And as I pondered, 'Lo,' I said, / 'When is the time? How may we know / The moment when to catch its flood / And yet avoid the undertow?'" (Brown, "How to Attain Your Good," 307). Brown was a member of the New Thought movement in the nineteenth century.

11. *Rocky Mountain Husbandman*, March 17, 1892.

12. "Home Colored Minstrel Company," Taylor Gordon and Rose Gordon Biography Project, August 6, 2008, https://taylorandrosegordonproject.wordpress.com/2008/08/06/home-colored-minstrel-company/.

13. Ivan Doig, a fellow resident of White Sulphur Springs, interviewed Gordon for a historical magazine that then neglected to publish it. Doig later found another way to write this story: by basing one of the main characters in his novel *Prairie Nocturne* (2003) on Gordon.

14. *Los Angeles Times*, July 18, 1937.

15. *Los Angeles Times*, July 9, 1937.

16. He was also in several western films, such as the all-black western *Two-Gun Man from Harlem* (1938).

17. Quoted in Anthony Wood, "Jess Lee Brooks: A Black Western Actor in the Narrative of the American West," *High Altitude History* (blog), May 17, 2017, https://historymsu.wordpress.com/2017/05/17/jess-lee-brooks-a-black-western-actor-in-the-narrative-of-the-black-west/.

18. See chapters 2 and 4.

19. See Smialkowska, "Shakespeare and 'Native Americans.'"

20. Fowler, "Oral Historian or Ethnologist?," 269.

21. See *Romeo and Juliet*, 2.2.43.

22. Dickson, *Worlds Elsewhere*, xv. Dickson's title is taken from Coriolanus's statement that "There is a world elsewhere" (*Coriolanus*, 3.3.145).

Chapter 5

1. Reprinted in *Great Falls Tribune*, December 6, 1948.

2. Montana Content Standards for English Language Arts and Literacy—K–12, Office of Public Instruction, 2017, http://montanateach.org/resources/montana-content-standards-for-english-language-arts-and-literacy-k-12/.

3. Doig, "One-Room America," ii.

4. *Butte Daily Inter-mountain*, March 8, 1899.

5. The West Side Shakespeare Club was excited to hear more from Eisenberg, thus they sponsored a series of lectures by him, during which he elucidated the plays, impersonated characters, and gave a controversial reading of Shylock as a vengeful Jew who was a by-product of his ill treatment at the hands of hypocritical Christians.

6. *Butte Daily Post*, September 21, 1903.

7. *Butte Miner*, June 1, 1904.

8. Charles Frey similarly notes, "By the time Shakespeare began to be introduced to the mass of American students in elocutionary readers, he was no longer regarded as a dramatist but rather as a writer of lofty moral tags." Frey, "Teaching Shakespeare in America," 544.

9. Burton, "Lay On, McGuffey," 97.

10. Catalog Fergus County Free High School, 1904, Montana Memory Project, https://mtmemory.org/.

11. *Searchlight*, April 30, 1909.

12. See the fuller account of Leiber in chapter 4.

13. *Bear Paw Mountaineer*, May 27, 1920.

14. See *Hamlet*, 2.2.300.

15. Writing in 1916, Franklin Thomas Baker surveyed the resistance to looking at Shakespeare as a playwright in nineteenth-century schools. He noted, however, that more recently a trend had emerged to "study [Shakespeare's] plays as drama written to be acted." Lower grades were beginning to dramatize the readings and upper grades to put on "a complete out-of-door performance of some Shakespearian play." Baker, "Shakespeare in the Schools," 38. Montana schools developed this approach as soon as, if not sooner than, those in the eastern United States.

16. For example, in 1892 a group of juniors from the Helena high school were reading *Othello*, "each undertaking a part." *Independent-Record*, February 21, 1892.

17. *Great Falls Tribune*, June 1, 1919.

18. *Big Timber Pioneer*, May 16, 1907.

19. *Roundup Record*, May 7, 1915. The allusion is to the lines from *King Lear:* "I am a man / More sinned against than sinning" (3.2.59–60).

20. *Great Falls Tribune*, June 18, 1916.

21. *Butte Miner*, November 25, 1909.

22. *Producers News*, March 21, 1919.

23. A long tradition of *Merchant of Venice* performances also showed Shylock as an overtly comic character.

24. There were other burlesques staged at this time as well, including two that were performed in Fort Benton. The *Hamlet* spoof was "The Lamentable Tragedy of Omelet and Oatmealia," featuring King Fraudius, Queen Milk, and a gravedigger named Toastem. Another burlesque was called "The Lamentable Tragedy of Julius Caesar" and included a character called Caesar's Cat. It was followed by a banquet that was a "strictly private affair" presided over by eighteen young ladies, one of whom was a "door keeper armed with a murderous looking hairpin" (*River Press*, May 19, 1909). Even in the 1880s, Fort Benton had an affinity for these spoofs, including a "musical travesty" of *Romeo and Juliet* (*River Press*, March 21, 1883).

25. The Dillon performance of this burlesque was reviewed in the *Dillon Tribune*, May 21, 1920.

26. Interestingly, however, *Merchant of Venice* is currently studied widely in schools in China.

27. See Wegner, *Lake County School History*, 234–35.

28. The fifth-grade classes in the Bozeman public elementary classes also routinely perform *A Midsummer Night's Dream*.

29. Chavala interview.

30. See *A Midsummer Night's Dream*, 5.1.239.

31. In 2019, Bozeman's Yellowstone Theological Institute also used *A Midsummer Night's Dream* as the foundation of its summer camp, showing students from the ages of nine to fourteen how to work together to create the "three worlds" of the play. The students had a chance to direct as well as to act in representative scenes from the play.

32. Belt Valley Shakespeare has performed *A Midsummer Night's Dream, As You Like It, Twelfth Night, 1 Henry IV, Tempest, Much Ado about Nothing*, and *Winter's Tale*.

33. Ross interview.

34. Ross, "Lessons from the Inside Out," 92. See interlude 1.

35. The Children's Shakespeare Society continues to be active, staging complex productions such as a 2019 full-length *Cymbeline* set in the Sami culture, with original music, costumes, set pieces, and cross-gender casting (directed by Sasha Kostyrko and Erik Pearson).

36. Students from the Belt Valley Shakespeare Players participated in the 2018 Montana Arts Integration Conference to speak about their Edinburgh experience, and the company returned to the fringe festival to perform *Winter's Tale* in 2019.

37. Moore correspondence.

38. *Dillon Examiner*, July 9, 1941.

39. *Normal College Index*, November 22, 1929.

40. *Normal College Index*, July 22, 1927.

41. *Butte Daily Post*, September 17, 1903.

42. *Montana Standard*, December 2, 1831.

43. Carroll College was founded in 1909 as Mount Saint Charles College and was renamed Carroll College in 1932.

44. *Prospector*, March 13, 1923.

45. The most significant legacy of Carroll College's investment in Shakespeare is that theatre instructor Kim DeLong developed a professional theatre organization in Helena called the Montana Shakespeare Company, which staged plays and ran a theatre camp for kids from 1997 until DeLong's untimely death in 2016.

46. *Prospector*, November 29, 1955.

47. Mansfield Library, University of Montana, Missoula.

48. *Great Falls Tribune*, February 4, 1962.

49. College of Great Falls newspaper, 1962, History Museum, Great Falls, Montana. An airman from the Malmstrom Air Force Base was even recruited to choreograph the fencing scenes.

50. *Exponent*, May 19, 1978.

Interlude 5

1. Hager, *Evelyn Cameron*, 6.
2. Cameron, 1922 journal, Montana Historical Society, Helena, Montana. See *Much Ado about Nothing*, 2.1.160–61.
3. Ivan Doig, "A Note to Readers," Ivan Doig website, ivandoig.com/notes.html.
4. Maclean, "USFS 1919," 176–77.
5. Maclean, 177.
6. Quoted in Pete Dexter, "The Old Man and the River: Pete Dexter's Classic Portrait of Norman Maclean," *Daily Beast*, April 14, 2017, https://www.thedailybeast.com/the-old-man-and-the-river-pete-dexters-classic-portrait-of-norma-maclean.
7. Quoted in Pete Dexter, "The Old Man and the River: Pete Dexter's Classic Portrait of Norman Maclean," *Daily Beast*, April 14, 2017, https://www.thedailybeast.com/the-old-man-and-the-river-pete-dexters-classic-portrait-of-norma-maclean.
8. Maclean, "Episode, Scene, Speech, and Word," 613. See also the analysis of Maclean's article by Weltzein, "Norman Maclean and Tragedy."
9. Tom Tollefson (Pete Dexter's brother, and the husband of Jane Moses, who was hired to type Maclean's book *Young Men and Fire*) made the same point about Maclean's primary interest in craft. See *Missoulian*, July 26, 2015 (article by Brett French).
10. Muir, "Among the Animals of the Yosemite," 130.
11. Muir, 132.
12. Hughes, "59th Bear," 94–95.

Chapter 6

1. *Clarion*, 1997 (quoting from a 1973 *Bozeman Daily Chronicle* article).
2. The updated mission statement of MSIP is "to engage and enrich both rural and underserved communities with professional productions of Shakespeare and other classics and, through educational outreach, to inspire creative expression and appreciation of the arts in young audiences." "About Shakespeare in the Parks," Montana Shakespeare in the Parks, www.shakespeareintheparks.org/about/overview.
3. That very same year (1977), a resident of Evergreen, Colorado, wrote to say that he had just happened to be staying a couple of weeks in Broadus when *Two Gentlemen of Verona* came to town. Much to this father's amazement, his twelve-year-old son, who had never seen Shakespeare before, was enthralled. MSIP's archives are full of letters like this, which serve as a testimony to the impact that the shows have across the age spectrum.
4. Chicago-based director and MSIP alumnus Bill Brown served as the associate director for a number of years. There was also a youth theatre camp associated with MSIP, run by MSU professor Stephanie Campbell. Meanwhile, Moira Keshishian took on the multiple roles of a marketer, grant writer, fund-raiser, and special events coordinator. Keshishian interview.

5. The winter productions directed by Asselin have included *Man of La Mancha, My Fair Lady, A Little Night Music, Death of a Salesman,* and *Noises Off.* As of 2019, the various MSIP programs are being performed over two hundred days a year.

6. See Warren, *Buffalo Bill's America,* 181–82.

7. *The Taming of the Shrew* has been performed six times during the summer season, not counting the excerpts performed during the 1973 season.

8. *Roundup Tribune,* August 9, 1989.

9. *Madisonian,* August 31, 1989.

10. *Clarion,* 2015.

11. *Clarion,* 2015.

12. *Missoulian,* July 14, 1989.

13. See *Taming of the Shrew,* 5.2.139.

14. Beehler and Steen, "Shakespeare in Montana 1989," 373.

15. Pullman had driven out west his second summer in college in a 1936 Dodge Coupe and picked up some work in South Dakota, just so he could be in this kind of landscape (Pullman interview).

16. *The Ballad of Lefty Brown* was filmed in Bannack, Dillon, Ennis, Whitehall, and Virginia City.

17. For an overview of the origins of outdoor Shakespeare in the United States, see Richard Paul, "How Shakespeare Ended Up in the Park," Public Radio International, May 23, 2019, https://www.pri.org/stories/2019–05–23/how-shakespeare-ended-park, and Georgianna Ziegler, "Outdoor Shakespeare: The Pioneers of a Summer Tradition," Folger Shakespeare Library, July 9, 2019, https://shakespeareandbeyond.folger.edu/2019/07/09/shakespeare-outdoor-pioneers-summer-tradition/?fbclid=IwAR0ELMmbL8BMfLjIJ-U_F4sumaANJE4PRT3qzRrUrlfhjZZbug1mPlHMjVM.

18. *Clarion,* 2006.

19. The allure of Montana's roads was for a long period enhanced by the fact that there was no daytime speed limit in the state until 1999.

20. *Montana Collegian,* Autumn 1973.

21. Quoted in Weiland and Wilsey, *State by State,* 263.

22. *Phoenix,* September 6, 1988, Montana Shakespeare in the Parks archives, Bozeman, Montana.

23. Denzin, "Performing Montana," 149.

24. *Montana Collegian,* Autumn 1973. See Figure 1 for a lightning storm on Poker Jim Butte.

25. Once Tom Morris fried an egg on the stage to prove that it was hot enough to do so (Jahnke interview).

26. Quoted in Golightly, Montana State University Research and Creativity publication.

27. Quotation from Debbie Lymon, Montana Shakespeare in the Parks archives, Bozeman, Montana.

28. McIntyre correspondence.

29. See *Macbeth,* 1.1.10.

30. See Minton, "'Season of All Natures,'" for a detailed look at the 2017 *Macbeth* production.
31. Denzin, "Performing Montana," 150.
32. Jahnke, *Clarion*, 2006.
33. Jahnke noted that one of the chief pleasures of the tour is that "[the actors] love the warm reception they experience in every venue, they love getting to know you and they love to share, however briefly, in the Montana experience" (*Clarion*, 1999).
34. *Exponent*, April 15, 1977.
35. One actor was thrilled when her homestay family in Fort Benton heeded her dietary restrictions and made her vegan cinnamon rolls. "In Montana, It's Shakespeare for Cowboys," *Backstage*, August 18, 2005, https://www.backstage.com/magazine/article/montana-shakespeare-cowboys-22055/.
36. Pullman interview.
37. Bennett, "Presence of Shakespeare," 219.
38. See prologue for comments about family by Matt Foss and the Fjells.
39. Kuntz interview.
40. In the MSIP thirtieth anniversary edition of the *Clarion*, a picture of a young boy with his family was explained with the following caption: "This picture was taken at our Great Falls performance in 1982. The man in the glasses is Dick Kuntz, chairman of our Shakespeare in the Schools advisory board. Sitting next to him is his wife, Dorothy, and his daughter Amy. The little boy is his son, Mark, who has been a favorite member of our acting companies . . . over the last several years" (*Clarion*, 2002). See also the article in *Great Falls Tribune*, August 1, 1996.
41. *Clarion*, 1998.
42. *Hamlet*, 2.2.189. "Not for an age, but for all time" comes from Ben Jonson's introductory poem, written for the publication of the Shakespeare First Folio in 1623.

Epilogue

1. Stephan Wolfert, "Mine Own Deformity: Shakespeare through the Lens of a Military Veteran," Howlround Theatre Commons, July 18, 2014, https://howlround.com/mine-own-deformity.
2. Bates, *Shakespeare Saved My Life*.
3. The National Endowment for the Arts' Shakespeare in American Communities program has partnered with the Departments of Defense and Justice to present plays on military bases and for youths in the justice system. Other Shakespeare programs for veterans and for the prison population are numerous.
4. Montana's first institution of higher learning was the Montana Collegiate Institute, founded in Deer Lodge in 1878.

BIBLIOGRAPHY

Archival Collections

Bannack State Park (Bannack)
Butte-Silver Bow Archives (Butte)
Dillon Public Library (Dillon)
The History Museum (Great Falls)
Kohrs Memorial Library (Deer Lodge)
Lewistown Public Library (Lewistown)
Montana Historical Society (Helena)
Montana Memory Project (https://mtmemory.org/)
Montana Shakespeare in the Parks (Bozeman)
Thompson-Hickman Madison Country Library (Virginia City)
University of Montana, Mansfield Library (Missoula)
Ursuline Academy (Great Falls)
Western Heritage Center (Billings)

Books, Articles, and Media

Adams, Kevin. *Class and Race in the Frontier Army: Military Life in the West, 1870–1890*. Norman: University of Oklahoma Press, 2009.

Albertson, Genevieve. "History of Shakespeare Club," compiled by Ethel Hawkins and Betty Henningsen. In *The History of Beaverhead County*, vol. 1, 585–86. Dillon, MT: Beaverhead County Museum, 1990.

Alter, J. Cecil. *Jim Bridger*. Norman: University of Oklahoma Press, 1962.

Ambrose, Stephen E. *Undaunted Courage: Meriwether Lewis, Thomas Jefferson, and the Opening of the American West*. New York: Touchstone, 1996.

Backroads of Montana. Episode 22, "Coming Home." Aired 2004, on PBS.

Baker, Franklin Thomas. "Shakespeare in the Schools." *Shakespearian Studies* (1916): 31–41.

Bard in the Backcountry: A Summer on the Road with Montana Shakespeare in the Parks, dir. Cindy Stillwell and Tom Watson. Hybrid Media LLC and Montana PBS, 2015.

Barsness, Larry. *Gold Camp: Alder Gulch and Virginia City, Montana.* New York: Hastings House, 1962.

Bates, Lauren. *Shakespeare Saved My Life: Ten Years in Solitary with the Bard.* Naperville, IL: Sourcebooks, Inc., 2013.

Beehler, Sharon, and Sara Jayne Steen. "Shakespeare in Montana 1989." *Shakespeare Quarterly* 41, no. 3 (1990): 372–74.

Behan, Barbara Carol. "Forgotten Heritage: African Americans in the Montana Territory, 1864–1889." *Journal of African American History* 91, no. 1 (2006): 23–40.

Bennett, Susan. "The Presence of Shakespeare." In *Shakespeare in Stages*, edited by Christie Carson and Christine Dymkowski, 210–28. Cambridge: Cambridge University Press, 2010.

Beran, Michael Knox. "Lincoln, *Macbeth*, and the Moral Imagination." *Humanitas* 11, no. 2 (1998). http://www.nhinet.org/beran.htm.

Blake, Henry Nichols. "Memoirs of a Many-Sided Man: The Personal Record of a Civil War Veteran, Montana Territory Editor, Attorney, Jurist," edited by Vivian A. Paladin. *Montana: The Magazine of Western History* 14, no. 4 (1964): 31–56.

Bourke, John G. *On the Border with Crook.* New York: Charles Scribner's Sons, 1891.

Briggeman, Kim, and Marcia Porter. "Daniel Edward Bandmann." ftp://ftp.ci.missoula.mt.us/Documents/Cemetery/Biographies/BANDMANN,%20Daniel.pdf

Brown, Henry Harrison. "How to Attain Your Good." *Now: The World's New Thought Journal* 15, no. 9 (1918): 303–8.

Burton, Jonathan. "Lay On, McGuffey: Excerpting Shakespeare in Nineteenth-Century Schoolbooks." In *Shakespearean Educations: Power, Citizenship, Performance*, edited by Coppélia Kahn, Heather S. Nathans, and Mimi Godfrey, 95–111. Newark: University of Delaware Press, 2011.

Carrell, Jennifer Lee. "How the Bard Won the West." *Smithsonian* 29 (1998): 99–107.

Carrington, Margaret Irvin. *Ab-sa-ra-ka, Land of Massacre: Being the Experience of an Officer's Wife on the Plains: With an Outline of Indian Operations and Conferences from 1865 to 1878.* Edited by Henry B. Carrington. Philadelphia: Lippincott, 1879.

Christie, J. W. "The Women's Clubs of Montana." *Rocky Mountain Magazine* 2, no. 1 (March 1901): 579–91.

Clark, Archie L. "John Maguire: Butte's 'Belasco.'" *Montana: The Magazine of Western History* 2, no. 1 (1952): 32–40.

Cochran, Alice. "The Gold Dust Trail: Jack Langrishe's Mining Town Theatres." *Montana: The Magazine of Western History* 20, no. 2 (1970): 58–69.

———. "Jack Langrishe and Theater on the Rocky Mountain Mining Frontier." Master's thesis, Southern Methodist University, 1968.

Coleman, Rufus A. "Daniel E. Bandmann, 'Shakespearean Stockman.'" *Montana: The Magazine of Western History* 4, no. 4 (1954): 32–34.

Cooper, James Fenimore. *Notions of the Americans.* 2 vols. London: Henry Colburn, 1828.

Croly, Jane C. *The History of the Women's Club Movement in America.* New York: Henry G. Allen & Co., 1898.

Davidson, Levette J. "Shakespeare in the Rockies." *Shakespeare Quarterly* 4, no. 1 (1953): 39–49.

Denzin, Norman K. "Performing Montana." In *Performance Ethnography: Critical Pedagogy and the Politics of Culture*, 148–63. New York: Sage, 2003.

Dickson, Andrew. *Worlds Elsewhere: Journeys around Shakespeare's Globe.* New York: Henry Holt and Co., 2015.

Dimsdale, Thomas J. *The Vigilantes of Montana, or Popular Justice in the Rocky Mountains.* Butte, MT: Mckee Printing Co., 1929.

Doig, Ivan. "One-Room America." Preface to Charlotte Caldwell, *Visions and Voices: Montana's One-Room Schoolhouses.* Clyde Park, MT: Barn Board Press, 2012.

———. *Sweet Thunder.* New York: Penguin, 2013.

Dunn, Esther Cloudman. *Shakespeare in America.* New York: Macmillan, 1939.

Eliel, Frank. *Southwestern Montana: Beaverhead Revisited.* New York: Finefrock Publishing, 1966.

Erskine, John. *The Memory of Certain Persons.* Philadelphia, PA: J. B. Lippincott, 1947.

Fellows, Virginia M. *The Shakespeare Code.* Gardiner, MT: Summit University Press, 2006.

Fowler, Loretta. "Oral Historian or Ethnologist? The Career of Bill Shakespeare." In *American Indian Intellectuals of the Nineteenth and Early Twentieth Centuries*, edited by Margot Liberty, 256–70. Norman: University of Oklahoma Press, 2002.

Frey, Charles. "Teaching Shakespeare in America." *Shakespeare Quarterly* 35, no. 5 (1984): 541–59.

Gere, Anne Ruggles. *Intimate Practices: Literacy and Cultural Work in U. S. Women's Clubs, 1880–1920.* Urbana: University of Illinois Press, 1997.

Golightly, Heather. Montana State University Research and Creativity publication, 1994.

Greenfield, Elizabeth. "Shakespearean 'Culture' in Montana, 1902." *Montana: The Magazine of Western History* 22, no. 2 (1972): 48–55.

Greenwald, Michael L. "Rough-Hewn Stages: Shakespeare and the American Frontier." *Shakespeare and Renaissance Association of the West Virginia* 8 (1983): 38–48.

Greever, William S. *The Bonanza West: The Story of the Western Mining Rushes, 1848–1900.* Norman: University of Oklahoma Press, 1963.

Hager, Kristi. *Evelyn Cameron: Montana's Frontier Photographer.* Helena, MT: Farcountry Press, 2007.

Hamilton, W. T. *My Sixty Years on the Plains: Trapping, Trading, and Indian Fighting.* Norman: University of Oklahoma Press, 1960.

Hanisch, Anika. *Stage Presence: How Two Theatre Companies Built Artistic Community and Brought Live Performance to the Rural West.* Bozeman, MT: Spiritus Creative, 2011.

Hosmer, Hezekiah. *Bacon and Shakespeare in the Sonnets.* San Francisco: Bancroft, 1887.

Hughes, Ted. "The 59th Bear." In *Birthday Letters.* New York: Farrar, Straus and Giroux, 1998.

Humfreville, J. Lee. *Twenty Years among Our Hostile Indians.* New York: Stackpole Books, 1874.

Knobloch, Margie Fjell. "Cultural Landscape of the Upper Tongue River Valley in Rosebud County, Montana." Helena, MT: Montana Preservation Alliance, 2007.

Koon, Helene. *How Shakespeare Won the West: Players and Performances in America's Gold Rush, 1849–65.* Jefferson, NC: McFarland, 1989.

L'Amour, Louis. *Hanging Woman Creek.* New York: Bantam Books, 1964

Lauterbach, Margaret McCutcheon, and Charles E. Lauterbach. *Comedian of the Frontier: The Life of Actor/Manager Jack Langrishe, 1825–1895.* Jefferson, NC: McFarland, 2016.

Levine, Lawrence W. *Highbrow/Lowbrow: The Emergence of Cultural Hierarchy in America.* Cambridge, MA: Harvard University Press, 1988.

———. "William Shakespeare and the American People: A Study in Cultural Transformation." In *Rethinking Popular Culture: Contemporary Perspectives in Cultural Studies,* edited by Chandra Mukerji and Michael Schudson, 157–97. Berkeley: University of California Press, 1991.

Lowe, Tom. *Bannack.* Dillon, MT: The Bannack Association.

Maclean, Norman. "Episode, Scene, Speech, and Word: The Madness of Lear." In *Critics and Criticism: Ancient and Modern,* edited by R. S. Crane, 595–615. Chicago: University of Chicago Press, 1952.

———. "USFS 1919: The Ranger, the Cook, and a Hole in the Sky." In *A River Runs Through It, and Other Stories,* 125–217. Chicago: University of Chicago Press, 1976.

Malone, Michael P., Richard B. Roeder, and William L. Lang. *Montana: A History of Two Centuries.* Seattle: University of Washington Press, 1976.

Malpas, Jeff. *Intelligence of Place: Topographies and Poetics.* London: Bloomsbury, 2015.

Marcy, R. B. *Thirty Years of Army Life on the Border.* Rev. ed. New York: J. B. Lippincott Company, 1963.

Marra, Kim. *Strange Duets: Impresarios and Actresses in the American Theatre, 1865–1914.* Iowa City: University of Iowa Press, 2006.

McCarthy, Cormac. *Blood Meridian, or The Evening Redness in the West.* New York: Vintage, 1985.

McClure, A. K. *Three Thousand Miles through the Rocky Mountains.* Philadelphia: J. B. Lippincott, 1869.

McRae, Wallace. *Stick Horses and Other Stories of Ranch Life.* Layton, UT: Gibbs Smith, 2009.

Milner, Clyde A., and Carol A. O'Connor. *As Big as the West: The Pioneer Life of Granville Stuart.* Oxford: Oxford University Press, 2009.

Minton, Gretchen E. "'The Season of All Natures': Montana Shakespeare in the Parks' Global Warming *Macbeth.*" *Shakespeare Bulletin* 36, no. 3 (2018): 429–48.

Montana Federation of Women's Clubs. Club Histories, District 11. 1964.

Muir, John. "Among the Animals of the Yosemite." Chap. 6 of *Our National Parks.* 1901; San Francisco: Sierra Club Books, 1991.

Nealy, E. B. "A Year in Montana." *Atlantic,* August 1866. https://www.theatlantic.com/magazine/archive/1866/08/a-year-in-montana/306241/.

Noyes, Al J. *In the Land of Chinook, or The Story of Blaine County.* Helena, MT: State Publishing Co., 1917.

Ogden, Dunbar H. *Theatre West: Image and Impact.* Atlanta: Rodopi, 1990.

Owen, Orville W. *Sir Francis Bacon's Cipher Story*, vol. 2. New York: Howard Publishing Co., 1894.

Pioneer Trails and Trials: Madison County, 1863–1920. Madison County History Association, 1976.

Porter, Esther. "A Compilation of Materials for a Study of the Early Theaters of Montana (1864–1880)." Master's thesis, University of Montana, 1938.

Roe, Fayette W. Scrapbook (1870), History Museum Archives, Great Falls, MT.

Rollins, Philip A. *The Cowboy.* New York: Charles Scribner's Sons, 1926.

Ronan, Mary, and Margaret Ronan. *Girl from the Gulches: The Story of Mary Ronan as Told to Margaret Ronan.* Edited by Ellen Baumler. Helena: Montana Historical Society Press, 2003.

Ross, Jeff. "Lessons from the Inside Out: Poetry, Epiphanies, and Creative Literary Culture in a Rural Montana High School." In *Literacy Teaching and Learning in Rural Communities: Problematizing Stereotypes, Challenging Myths*, edited by Lisa Schade Eckert and Janet Alsup, 78–94. New York: Routledge, 2015.

Russell, Osborne. *Journal of a Trapper.* Edited by Aubrey L. Haines. Lincoln: University of Nebraska Press, 1955.

Scheil, Katherine West. *She Hath Been Reading: Women and Shakespeare Clubs in America.* Ithaca, NY: Cornell University Press, 2012.

Shapiro, James. *Contested Will: Who Wrote Shakespeare?* New York: Simon and Schuster, 2010.

———. *Shakespeare in America: An Anthology from the Revolution to Now.* New York: The Library of America, 2014.

Smialkowska, Monika. "Shakespeare and 'Native Americans': Forging Identities through the 1916 Tercentenary." *Critical Survey* 22, no. 2 (2010): 76–90.

Stanley, David, and Elaine Thatcher, eds. *Cowboy Poets and Cowboy Poetry.* Urbana: University of Illinois Press, 2000.

Stiles, T. J. *Custer's Trials: A Life on the Frontier of a New America.* New York: Vintage, 2015.

Stuart, Granville. *Diary and Sketchbook of a Journey to "America" in 1866, & Return Trip up the Missouri River to Fort Benton, Montana.* Los Angeles: Dawson's Book Shop, 1963.

———. *Forty Years on the Frontier, as Seen in the Journals and Reminiscences of Granville Stuart*, vol. 1. Edited by Paul. C Phillips. Cleveland: Arthur H. Clark, 1925.

Sturgess, Kim. *Shakespeare and the American Nation.* Cambridge: Cambridge University Press, 2004.

Tocqueville, Alexis de. *Democracy in America*, vol. 2. New York: Alfred A Knopf, Inc., 1994.

Tubbs, Stephenie Ambrose. *The Lewis and Clark Companion: An Encyclopedic Guide to the Voyage of Discovery.* New York: Macmillan, 2003.

———. "Turn-of-the-Century Women's Clubs in America." Master's thesis, University of Montana, 1986.

van Orman, Richard A. "The Bard in the West." *Western Historical Quarterly* 5, no. 1 (1974): 34–35.

Vaughan, Alden T., and Virginia Mason Vaughan. *Shakespeare in America*. Oxford: Oxford University Press, 2012.

Victor, Frances Fuller. *The River of the West: The Adventures of Joe Meek*. Vol 1, *The Mountain Years*. Edited by Winfred Blevins. Missoula, MT: Mountain Press Publishing Co, 1983.

Warde, Frederick. *Fifty Years of Make-Believe*. New York: International Press Syndicate, 1920.

Warhank, Josef J. "Fort Keogh: Cutting Edge of a Culture." Master's thesis, California State University, Long Beach, 1983.

Warren, Louis S. *Buffalo Bill's America*. New York: Alfred A. Knopf, 2005.

Wegner, Joyce Decker. *Lake County School History*, vol. 1. Edited by Jennifer Groneberg. Stevensville, MT: Stoneydale Publishing Company, 2010.

Weiland, Matt, and Sean Wilsey. *State by State: A Panoramic Portrait of America*. New York: Harper Collins, 2008.

Weltzein, O. Alan. "Norman Maclean and Tragedy." *Western American Literature* 30, no. 2 (1995): 139–49.

Wister, Owen. *The Virginian: A Horseman of the Plains*. Rev. ed. New York: Penguin, 1988.

Works by Shakespeare

All quotations from Shakespeare's works are taken from the Arden Shakespeare, Third Series. *Shakespeare in Montana* includes quotations from the following plays:

Antony and Cleopatra, ed. John Wilders (1995)

As You Like It, ed. Juliet Dusinberre (2006)

Coriolanus, ed. Peter Holland (2013)

Cymbeline, ed. Valerie Wayne (2017)

Hamlet, ed. Ann Thomson and Neil Taylor (2006)

Henry IV, Part 1, ed. David Scott Kastan (2002)

Henry V, ed. T. W. Craik (1995)

Henry VI, Part 2, ed. Ronald Knowles (1999)

Julius Caesar, ed. David Daniell (1998)

King Lear, ed. R. A. Foakes (1997)

Macbeth, ed. Sandra Clark and Pamela Mason (2015)

Measure for Measure, ed. A. R. Braunmuller and Robert N. Watson (2020)

The Merchant of Venice, ed. John Drakakis (2011)

The Merry Wives of Windsor, ed. Giorgio Melchiori (1999)

A Midsummer Night's Dream, ed. Sukanta Chaudhuri (2017)

Much Ado about Nothing, ed. Claire McEachern (2006)

Othello, ed. E. A. J. Honigmann (1997)

Richard II, ed. Charles Forker (2002)

Richard III, ed. James R. Siemon (2009)

Romeo and Juliet, ed. René Weis (2012)

Sonnets, ed. Katherine Duncan-Jones (2010)
The Taming of the Shrew, ed. Barbara Hodgdon (2010)
The Tempest, ed. Virginia Mason Vaughan and Alden T. Vaughan (2011)
Timon of Athens, ed. Anthony B. Dawson and Gretchen E. Minton (2008)
Troilus and Cressida, ed. David Bevington (1998)
Twelfth Night, ed. Keir Elam (2008)
Two Gentlemen of Verona, ed. William Carroll (2004)
The Winter's Tale, ed. John Pitcher (2010)

Newspapers and Magazines

(All towns are in Montana unless otherwise noted.)
Anaconda Standard (Butte-Anaconda)
Bear Paw Mountaineer (Big Sandy)
Big Timber Pioneer (Big Timber)
Billings Gazette (Billings)
Bozeman Daily Chronicle (Bozeman)
Butte Daily Inter-mountain (Butte)
Butte Daily Post (Butte)
Butte Miner (Butte)
Butte Semi-weekly Miner (Butte)
Central City Weekly Register-Call (Central City, CO)
Clarion (Montana Shakespeare in the Parks annual magazine)
Daily Missoulian (Missoula)
Dillon Examiner (Dillon)
Dillon Tribune (Dillon)
Exponent (Montana State University, Bozeman)
Glasgow Courier (Glasgow)
Great Falls Tribune (Great Falls)
Helena Weekly Herald (Helena)
Independent-Record (Helena)
Iola Register (Iola, KS)
Kendall Miner (Kendall)
Livingston Enterprise (Livingston)
Los Angeles Times (Los Angeles, CA)
Madisonian (Virginia City)
Missoula Weekly Gazette (Missoula)
Missoulian (Missoula)
Montana Collegian (Montana State University, Bozeman)
Montana Post (Virginia City)
Montana Standard (Butte)
Montana Woman (Montana Federation of Women's Clubs)
Montreal Gazette (Montreal, Canada)

New York Clipper (New York, NY)
New York Times (New York, NY)
Normal College Index (Dillon)
Producers News (Plentywood)
Prospector (Carroll College, Helena)
River Press (Fort Benton)
Rocky Mountain Husbandman (Diamond City)
Rocky Mountain News (Denver, CO)
Roundup Record (Roundup)
Roundup Tribune (Roundup)
Searchlight (Culbertson)
Semi-weekly Billings Gazette (Billings)
Yellowstone Journal and Live Stock Reporter (Miles City)
Yellowstone Monitor (Glendive)

Personal Interviews and Correspondence

Asselin, Kevin. Personal Interview. February 5, 2016.
Chavala, Stephanie. Personal Interview. April 1, 2017.
Dickerson, Will. Personal Interview. January 15, 2016.
Foss, Matt. Personal Correspondence. January 16, 2016.
Hagen, Cindy. Personal Interview. July 6, 2019.
Hosking, John. Personal Interview. August 4, 2017.
Jahnke, Joel. Personal Interview. January 13, 2016.
Keshishian, Moira. Personal Interview. August 8, 2018.
Kuntz, Mark. Personal Interview. August 1, 2018.
McIntyre, Doug. Personal Correspondence. July 19, 2018.
Moore, Johanna. Personal Correspondence. June 26, 2019.
Morris, Tom. Personal Interview. January 27, 2016.
Pullman, Bill. Personal Interview. January 19, 2018.
Reierson, Elizabeth. Personal Correspondence. January 24, 2016.
Richards, Michael. Personal Correspondence. January 25, 2016.
Ross, Jeff. Personal Interview. March 12, 2017
Smith, Rhonda. Personal Interview. January 27, 2016.
Walton, Kelsey. Personal Correspondence. January 29, 2016.

INDEX